THE LOSE YOUR GUT GUIDE

THE WORKOUT, MEAL PLAN, AND MIND-SET YOU NEED TO DITCH YOUR SPARE TIRE AND GET LEAN

By Dezi Abeyta, RDN
and the editors of
Men's Health

This book is intended as a reference volume only, not as a medical manual. The information given here is designed to help you make informed decisions about your health. It is not intended as a substitute for any treatment that may have been prescribed by your doctor. If you suspect that you have a medical problem, we urge you to seek competent medical help.

Mention of specific companies, organizations, or authorities in this book does not imply endorsement by the author or publisher, nor does mention of specific companies, organizations, or authorities imply that they endorse this book, its author, or the publisher.

Internet addresses and telephone numbers given in this book were accurate at the time it went to press.

© 2021 by Hearst Magazines, Inc.

All rights reserved. No part of this publication may be reproduced or transmitted in any form or by any means, electronic or mechanical, including photocopying, recording, or any other information storage and retrieval system, without the written permission of the publisher.

Men's Health is a registered trademark of Hearst Magazines, Inc.

Cover Photography © Mike Garten: front and back

Interior Photography

© Lauren Adkisson: 6; © Georgijevic/Getty Images: 7; © d3sign/Getty Images: 8; © Westend61/Getty Images: 10, 22; © mixetto/Getty Images: 12; © Geber86/Getty Images: 15; © Asia-Pacific Images Studio/Getty Images: 16; © Constantinis/Getty Images: 18; © visualspace/Getty Images: 29; © PeopleImages/Getty Images: 30, 68; © svetikd/Getty Images: 34; © Altan Can/EyeEm/Getty Images: 38; © Tashi-Delek/Getty Images: 39; © PhotoAlto/Getty Images: 43; © VioletaStoimenova/Getty Images: 45; © eclipse_images/Getty Images: 50; © Mikolette/Getty Images: 52; © Nikada/Getty Images: 55; © Alexander Spatari/Getty Images: 56; © isetiana/Getty Images: 61; © Claudia Totir/Getty Images: 63; © Arx0nt/Getty Images: 64; © The Picture Pantry/Getty Images: 67; © 10,000 Hours/Getty Images: 71; © Lori Andrews/Getty Images: 73; © Cavan Images/Getty Images: 76; © Tom Werner/Getty Images: 78; © Mike Garten: 79-125; © gradyreese/Getty Images: 126; © Kat Wirsing: 128-131; © Paul Aresu/Getty Images: 132; © Savannah Case: 135

Book design by Kim Gray

Library of Congress Cataloging-in-Publication Data is on file with the publisher.

ISBN 978-1-950099-78-8

2 4 6 8 10 9 7 5 3 1 paperback
HEARST

THE LOSE YOUR GUT GUIDE

CONTENTS

PART ONE

Why It's Time to Battle Belly Fat

CHAPTER 1: **The Dangers of Belly Fat....8**

CHAPTER 2: **What Causes Belly Fat....19**

PART TWO

How to Lose It for Good

CHAPTER 3: **Maximize the Way You Move....31**

CHAPTER 4: **Fuel Your Body for Fat Burning....45**

CHAPTER 5: **Get Your Mind-Set Right....52**

PART THREE

The Tools

CHAPTER 6: **The Meal Plan....56**

CHAPTER 7: **The Workout....127**

CHAPTER 8: **The Mind-Set....132**

CONTENTS

127

108

RECIPES

Spicy Quinoa Tacos.....**80**
Overnight Blueberry Oat Success....**82**
Protein Breakfast Power Bowl....**85**
Delicious Tofu Shakshuka....**86**
Chocolate Protein Pancakes....**88**
Anti-Inflammatory Chicken Salad....**91**
Shrimp Zoodle Stir-Fry....**92**
PB&J Overnight Oats....**95**
Taco Breakfast Bowl....**97**
Banana Nut Pancakes....**98**
Greek Chicken Salad....**101**
Asian Pork Lettuce Wraps....**102**
Ground Beef, Asparagus, and Mashed Sweet Potatoes....**104**
Cajun Shrimp Penne....**105**
Breakfast Taco Nachos....**107**
Lemon Tart Smoothie....**108**
Popcorn Chicken & Coconut Zucchini Fries....**110**
Blackened Fish Taco Bowls....**111**
Paleo Overnight Oats....**113**
Brownie Protein Pancakes....**114**
One-Pan Hawaiian Salmon....**117**
One-Pan Lamb Meatballs & Veggies....**119**
One-Pan Chicken Stir-Fry....**120**
Slow-Cooker Beef Stew....**123**
Grilled Shrimp Salad....**124**

Introduction

WHY YOU NEED YOUR WHY

This project is more than a push for you to lose weight. The weight itself is simply a metric. What I'm asking you to do is to learn how to lose the weight of stress. The weight of diminishing confidence that keeps you from sleeping with your partner or perhaps asking for that promotion. I'm asking you to lose the weight of loneliness that comes with the isolation stemming from not loving yourself enough to move more, to eat better, and to actually take time toward self-development. This plan will teach you how to lose that pesky belly fat, but it's meant to do so much more.

As a registered dietitian specializing in men's health, I can't tell you how many times I've talked with a man who has lost himself. Sure, he's contacted me for his fat-loss goals, but what he's truly searching for is a way to connect with his partner again and to feel confident about his naked body. I mean, we all want that, right? That same guy wants to also submit a legacy that he's proud of. He sees what his parents couldn't teach him and also how his kids are starting to struggle with their own health at such a young age, and he's scared because he wants to be there for his grandkids and wants his kids to be there for theirs. But you know what? This same guy is incredibly capable and at the same time culpable. While it would be easy to place blame, it goes deeper than that. Most of the men that I've worked with lack purpose. They lack their "why" — it's not that they don't have time, or money, or energy. It's that they don't know why they're doing what they're doing.

This project is meant to teach you the information but, even more so, the application. So, sit down with an open mind, be willing to audit your behaviors and your mind-set, and be willing to try something uncomfortable because what has been comfortable has gotten you to a point where you are needing to read this book. Take messy action and let's get to work. You got this!

—Dezi Abeyta, RDN, founder of Foodtalk Nutrition

PART 1

Belly fat is about more than appearances. The causes of it—stress, unhealthy diet, poor sleep hygiene, and lack of exercise, to name a few— have effects beyond your belt, and the consequences of it can literally cut your life short. Luckily, it's never been easier to get rid of it once and for all.

WHY IT'S TIME TO
BATTLE BELLY FAT

Chapter 1

THE DANGERS OF BELLY FAT

In spite of this chapter's name, we're not here to completely bust you on the extra inches that may have crept up around your waistline recently. It would be unfair to launch into the increased disease risks and hormonal issues and everything else without first saying: Belly fat isn't your fault (well, not totally). It's a beast of an enemy that's way too easy to summon.

CHAPTER 1 | The Dangers of Belly Fat

As a guy, you are unfortunately very likely to have it. Your stomach is often the first place fat settles. Hormones and genetics conspire to make it that way. Also, a bulging belly can seemingly happen out of nowhere, especially as you get older. With age comes a slower metabolism, the process by which your body converts food into energy. As it becomes less efficient, it has more trouble turning Friday-night pizza into something usable; and in general, you're more likely to start storing fat and losing willpower. Add to that the endless opportunities for greasy or boozy or sugary things in your diet, and it can feel like belly fat is unavoidable.

So, whatever your story is of how you got your gut, know that it's normal. And know that Dezi Abeyta, RDN, the expert whose belly-busting secrets you're about to read, has heard all those stories from his clients and helped every single one change for the better. Maybe you feel like you haven't changed your daily routine at all, and now all of a sudden your favorite tee is tight. Or maybe you paused your 4-days-a-week gym sessions for what felt like a minute only to see your hard work poof into a bigger waistline, thus diminishing confidence. Or maybe you've been consistently clocking workouts for months and dropping minimal pounds only to find that your belly fat has yet to change.

The plus side to all this is that no matter how your gut got there, there is a no-fail way to make it go away. But before we tell you how to do that, there actually is one reason you might want (some) to stay. Body fat in general isn't all bad. Believe it or not, it serves the noble purpose of helping you survive every single day in a number of critical ways. Fat actually insulates your body from the cold and the heat. It cushions your internal organs from outside damage. It serves as your emergency fuel source when your blood sugar runs out. Even your brain needs it: A minimum of 60 percent of your brain is actually made from fat. It's the fattiest organ in your body! Basically, you wouldn't be the person you are today if it weren't for fat, because it plays a role in nearly every single biological function in your body. To put it simply, fat is impossible to live without.

009

Benefits of Fat

Like we said, it's not all bad. Guys need around 2 to 5 percent of their weight to be from essential fat. This type of fat is necessary for:

ENERGY

MAINTAINING PROPER HORMONE LEVELS

REGULATING BODY TEMPERATURE

PROTECTING VITAL ORGANS

FERTILITY

BONE GROWTH

A little will do your body good. Too much can seriously start to tax your heart and other organs.

Of course, it doesn't take much to go from having the essential amount of fat to an unhealthy amount. And studies show that while general obesity is unhealthy, carrying excess body fat specifically around your belly is even worse. So, what exactly does a little extra weight around the waist do to your health? Here are just some of the ways it can put you at risk.

INCREASED RISK OF HEART DISEASE

Heart disease is the leading cause of death in American men (as well as the biggest killer of women). It was the cause of 1 out of every 4 male deaths in the country in 2017, according to the Centers for Disease Control and Prevention (CDC). It can happen at any age, and it is becoming increasingly common in guys under 40, says a 2019 study from the American College of Cardiology.

Heart disease actually refers to several different types of heart conditions, and not all result in a heart attack. Coronary heart disease is the most common and is the result of plaque buildup in your

CHAPTER 1 | The Dangers of Belly Fat

arteries, which are responsible for pumping blood to your heart. Without a clear passageway, blood can't flow as easily to your heart. Ultimately, this restricted flow can trigger chest pain, a heart attack, or sudden cardiac arrest.

The dangerous thing about heart disease is that you may not know you have symptoms until a heart attack hits. But you do have one major alarm staring you right in the face: belly fat. Extra weight around your middle has been linked to an increased risk of heart disease for a couple of reasons. For one, it may actually release chemicals that lead to inflammation, which can cause build-ups in your arteries to break off, wedge into arteries farther downstream, and impair blood flow to your heart. For another, belly fat is most often made of visceral fat. This specific type of fat protects your internal organs, so a little isn't bad. But too much has been linked to an increased risk of health issues, including heart disease. Other factors, like smoking and stress, also up your chance of cardiac issues, so you'll want to focus on minimizing all risks to keep your heart in optimal shape.

INCREASED RISK OF DIABETES

Like heart conditions, the symptoms of diabetes can be easy to miss, especially in prediabetes and type 2 diabetes, the most common form of the disease. According to the CDC's *2020 National Diabetes Statistics Report*, 7.2 million adults who had diabetes didn't even realize it. The problem with not realizing it: It's the number 6 killer of men in America, according to the CDC. This chronic condition, which is characterized by elevated blood sugar levels, can lead to long-term issues with vision, memory, and wound healing, plus serious ailments like kidney disease, heart disease, or even cancer. But there is something you can do to help prevent it, and that's get your gut in check. Wider waistlines have been strongly linked to an increased risk of type 2 diabetes and prediabetes, which is the precursor to type 2 diabetes.

The belly–diabetes connection comes back to visceral fat, the hidden layer of fat that lives beneath muscle. It's been shown to contribute to insulin resistance, which is often a signal that you're

THE LOSE YOUR GUT GUIDE

headed toward prediabetes. Insulin lowers the amount of sugar in your bloodstream by allowing sugar, or glucose, into your cells. But when you're insulin resistant, this efficient shuttling of sugar from your bloodstream to your cells stops. Instead, your body increases production of insulin, and the sugar builds up in your bloodstream. If this goes on for too long, it can trigger chronic elevation of blood sugar, which can result in full-blown diabetes.

CHAPTER 1 | The Dangers of Belly Fat

The Two Types of Belly Fat

The extra weight around your middle actually comes in two different forms: subcutaneous and visceral. Here's how each can impact your health.

SUBCUTANEOUS FAT

Most simply and unscientifically put, this is the fat you can see, the stuff you can actually grab. The word subcutaneous literally breaks apart to "beneath" (sub) "the skin" (cutaneous). This variety of fat is totally visible and is found all over the body—from your stomach to the tips of your fingers. This is also the kind of fat that you need to survive. You need a little subcutaneous fat to provide things such as energy and insulation during colder months. But having too much of it can be a visible sign that a person is overweight or obese, both of which are known to raise the risk for many diseases, including heart disease, stroke, metabolic syndrome, certain types of cancer, type 2 diabetes, and sleep apnea.

VISCERAL FAT

The second type of fat is the more harmful kind. Visceral fat is found deep within the torso, and although some visceral fat is needed to protect the organs around the abdomen, too much can lead to big trouble. In fact, because of its proximity to your kidneys, heart, liver, and other organs, excess visceral fat can raise your risk of all sorts of diseases, from heart disease and diabetes to cancer and Alzheimer's. It's sometimes referred to as "hidden" belly fat because you can't see it from the outside.

THE LOSE YOUR GUT GUIDE

INCREASED RISK OF DEMENTIA

A bigger belly doesn't just impact your physical health. A 2019 study in *Obesity* found a link between abdominal fat and the potential to develop dementia, which includes a group of conditions that cause everything from memory loss to degraded social skills. And a 2017 report in the *Journal of Alzheimer's Disease* showed that insulin resistance, which belly fat makes you more susceptible to, may also be a factor in dementia risk. The researchers found that patients in the highest quartile for insulin resistance had the worst cognitive performance, whether or not they were diabetic. They also had poorer memory, executive function (the ability to perform

tasks requiring conscious, deliberate thought), and quicker mental decline. More than 5 million Americans over the age of 65 are currently living with Alzheimer's, according to the Alzheimer's Association *2020 Alzheimer's Disease Facts and Figures*; and although treatments have been developed to help ease the severity of symptoms, there is no cure.

HORMONAL ISSUES

Hormones are critically important to your daily functioning. They're your body's messaging system. They tell other parts of your body what to do. When one gets out of whack, it can often impact others. And the size of your gut can throw a wrench into the whole system, particularly in regard to your testosterone levels. Studies have shown that greater amounts of visceral fat are connected to lower amounts of testosterone in guys. As many as 5 million men in the United States (generally older men) do have low levels of this hormone. Symptoms include erectile problems, lack of energy (never feeling rested, no matter what you do), and an AWOL libido. It also can mess with your weight,

BRAIN DRAIN

One 2019 study found that participants with high BMIs and waist-to-hip ratios had less gray matter in the brain, which is responsible for functions like self-control and muscle control.

014

THE LOSE YOUR GUT GUIDE

making this a frustrating cycle. When testosterone levels are good, they help build muscle. Testosterone signals for the muscle-building process to commence, spurring satellite cells into action. The more muscle you have, the more calories you can burn at rest. But a low T supply makes this process way harder, which can translate to trouble dropping pounds.

HOW MUCH IS TOO MUCH?

To recap: You need some belly fat to live but not too much, or it'll sabotage your health. That's a lot of gray area, especially since most guys gain belly fat gradually, a pound here and a pound there. When does it cross the line? You might assume it's when your weight is classified as overweight, which the CDC defines as having a body mass index (BMI)

somewhere in the range of 25 to 30. BMI is calculated using a formula that factors in your height and weight. But these numbers don't tell the entire story here and are rarely regarded as highly as waist circumference. The National Institutes of Health notes that guys who have a waist circumference greater than 40 inches are at a higher risk of diabetes and heart disease—no matter the number on the scale. That is the same number the American Heart Association (AHA) uses to diagnose someone with abdominal obesity. Although your belly circumference is an important factor, there are risks associated with being overweight in general, even if your waistline clocks in under 40 inches. Aim to achieve both a healthy BMI and waist circumference. You can determine the latter with a simple tape measure.

Take Note

To measure your belly properly, run a tape measure around your waist, just above the hip bone (not necessarily where your belt usually is, which may have migrated below that). Relax, exhale, and measure without sucking your belly in. It's useful to record the number so you can see how it changes when you lose weight.

CHAPTER 1 | The Dangers of Belly Fat

Figuring out your BMI is a little more involved. The CDC breaks BMI down into four categories. If your BMI is 25 or higher, you're considered to be overweight; and if it's 30 or above, you're classified as obese. Your health is at greatest risk if your BMI is 40 or more, because this is considered morbidly obese. Too low a BMI isn't good either. A BMI below 18.5 is considered underweight, indicating that you have too low a percentage of body fat to ensure healthy functioning. What you want is a number between 18.5 and 24.9. However, it's important to remember that other factors can play a role in what constitutes an unhealthy weight, and in most cases, taking a look at the full picture is going to be your best tool.

Whether you do it for your heart, your hormones, or that feeling of fitting back into your favorite jersey, dropping pounds around your waistline will benefit your life in countless ways. You'll decrease your risk of life-threatening diseases, improve your overall hormone functioning, and generally feel better. With the guidance in this book, you'll be able to get rid of your gut once and for all—and without totally blowing up your life. We show you the smart and easy tweaks you can make to your life to start losing pounds fast.

Chapter 2

WHAT CAUSES BELLY FAT

Before jumping into the gut-busting 3-week meal plan, workout, and lifestyle changes laid out in this guide, it helps to understand why it works—why it is the only real way to finally achieve body re-composition. If you've found that you haven't been able to lose your gut no matter what you do, this will explain

THE LOSE YOUR GUT GUIDE

why. The plan works for two main reasons: It directly addresses the causes of belly fat (which we outline in this chapter), and it does so in a way that doesn't suck the fun out of life. You will still be able to eat things with the word brownie in them, and you won't need to spend an hour in the gym every day. It's about practical changes.

So, let's look at what is causing you to hold weight in your belly. There is no single food or lifestyle factor that sends a signal to your body to start piling the pounds directly onto your gut. Just like you can't exactly direct all your weight-loss efforts to reducing fat in just one part of your body, you can't quite eat one type of food or engage in one type of activity to gain weight in a specific area either. It's true that drinking too many brews can lead to the proverbial "beer belly," but belly fat isn't solely caused by an excess of alcohol. Or fried foods. Or even too much couch time. Instead, many different factors collude to puff up your gut. Some you can control, and others are simply facts of life. For the fixed variables, like aging, although you can't pause the clock, you can learn to

strategically deal with its effects. And for the factors you can control, we will show you exactly how to adjust your habits to keep things like sleep, overeating, and stress in check.

WHY IT ALL GOES RIGHT TO YOUR GUT

Think about the moment when you realized you had put on a few extra pounds. More likely than not, the first place it showed up was at your waistline, causing your shirt to bunch, your belt to bulge. This makes weight gain ridiculously easy to write off. Whose belly doesn't protrude after mozzarella sticks, fries, a burger, and a beer from your local casual eatery? But it's not a temporary illusion. Your midsection is the first place fat tends to go.

As a guy, you are built to store excess weight in your gut before any other part of your body. You're just naturally disadvantaged when it comes to where you put on pounds. Men and women typically gain excess weight differently, with guys being more prone to packing on the pounds around the waist. Female body fat, on the other hand, often

020

CHAPTER 2 | **What Causes Belly Fat**

concentrates around the hips, thighs, and buttocks. Men actually have twice as much fat around the abdominal cavity (or less scientifically put, around the stomach) as women. Hormones may be partly to blame for this disparity. Lower-body fat cells are more responsive to the hormone estrogen, found in higher levels in women; whereas abdominal fat is more responsive to the stress hormone adrenaline. Another reason for this difference may be related to a gene that codes for lipoprotein lipase (LPL), an enzyme made by fat cells to help store calories as fat. In women, fat cells in the hips, breasts, and thighs release LPL, while in men it's produced by fat cells in the belly area. Women are also more likely to store fat as subcutaneous fat rather than visceral fat, though they start storing visceral fat when they reach menopause. In a nutshell, as a guy, you are destined to hold more fat in your belly and more of the dangerous kind.

So, what is causing your body to hang on to all this fat in the first place? Let's start with the factors that are out of your hands. Genetics do play a role in the size of your gut, but perhaps not as much as

you might think. Your genes can impact your chances of being overweight or obese as well as where this extra fat ends up on your body. For example, changes in the MC4R gene can end up making you feel very hungry and as a result cause you to consume more calories than you need. More food than you need = a higher chance of gaining weight. A 2014 study identified three genes that are related to waist-to-hip ratio (WHR), a measure that indicates how much belly fat you have, though more than 50 genes have been linked to obesity. Their impact has been shown to be rather small; however, they can make a difference.

The aging process can also tip the scales in favor of more fat, particularly around your midsection. You will lose muscle as you get older. It's part of a condition that happens to pretty much everyone called sarcopenia. When you lose muscle, it can very easily result in fat gain. But how much you lose and when you start losing it are very much under your control. The best defense against sarcopenia is to build as much muscle as you can and then work every day to retain it. Getting

CHAPTER 2 | What Causes Belly Fat

older also can mean becoming more prone to injuries and taking longer to bounce back from them. And as you might guess, being sidelined from physical activity is never good for your waistline. Even without injuries, as you get older, your work capacity starts to decline along with your ability to recuperate from the work you put in. Those of us in middle age simply can't go 110 percent every time we walk into the gym and expect to recover like we could 10 or 20 years ago.

If there are so many natural, unavoidable elements pushing us toward a bigger waistline, why don't all guys have a gut? Enter your lifestyle: your day-to-day choices about the things you do and how you respond to the things that happen to you. Think about it in terms of aging. While muscle mass naturally decreases with age, as you get older, you also tend to cut back on physical activity. You're likely to eat a little more and work out a lot less. Considering that muscle loss slows the rate at which your body burns calories, these unhealthy habits are a surefire way to pack on the pounds. And if you're not limiting your

caloric intake or upping your workouts as you age, chances are you'll gain weight. The same thing can happen while you're young. The good news is your lifestyle is easier to change than you think.

WHAT YOU CAN CONTROL

Aging, genetics, and hormones may be pretty much set in stone, but the factors that contribute the most to a big stomach are totally in your court. When you address these, you can start dropping pounds. Take a look at the lifestyle factors that trigger belly fat listed in the following pages. Note which ones sound most like your daily life. These are what you will want to direct most of your energy toward.

Your Stress Level

Unlike acute stress, which has a beginning and an end, chronic stress is ongoing. This is what makes chronic stress dangerous. When your job is on shaky ground, your marriage hits a rough patch, your bank account is dwindling, your aging parents suddenly need a lot more care—or all of these things happen at once!—that is chronic stress. (It may

THE LOSE YOUR GUT GUIDE

seem counterintuitive, but chronic stress can also result from positive things. While landing a new job, getting married, or having a baby is each an exciting life event, they're also different than what you're used to, so they can cause stress.) The problem is your body still reacts as if these stresses were acute, yet—and here's the important distinction—there's no calming period.

When you are chronically stressed, your sympathetic nervous system (SNS) just keeps doing its stuff, keeping you in a state of heightened physiological arousal as if your very life were being threatened all the time, every day. During such a state, your digestive system slows down and insulin production ramps up, overriding signals from adrenaline to burn fat, and encouraging your body to store it in anticipation of future needs. Your body's reaction to stress is to actually hold on to fat instead of burning it. During times of stress, you're also less likely to make gut-healthy decisions like eating micronutrient-rich fruits and vegetables or going for a jog, so a rough week can do a double whammy on your waistline. The more your body's stress

Stress Eat to Lose Weight

When the day has got you frazzled, you're more likely to nosh to distract yourself. If you eat nutrient-rich and wholesome foods, you can actually lower your stress levels. Here's what to eat to calm the eff down:

BERRIES: They're packed with vitamin C, which has been shown to lower cortisol levels.

CASHEWS: Low levels of zinc have been linked to anxiety. Get your fix with a handful of this plant-based protein.

CHAMOMILE TEA: Study after study shows this herb has powerful calming effects.

DARK CHOCOLATE: It's been associated with lower blood pressure, which can make you feel at ease.

OATMEAL: This complex carb triggers serotonin production, aka the feel-good chemical.

CHAPTER 2 | What Causes Belly Fat

response system is activated, the harder it is to switch off. And that's a major concern, given that anywhere from 60 to 90 percent of illness is stress-related.

Your Diet

It may seem obvious on paper, but it's ridiculously easy to consume more calories than you think you are. Grocery store shelves are lined with snacks and beverages that are much more calorie-rich than they might appear. Packaged treats often come with multiple servings, though that's easy to forget when you're sitting on the couch in the middle of bingeing your favorite show. The potential to overeat can be even greater if you worked out. After all, you definitely feel like you burned 1,000 calories after a 45-minute run, but in most instances, that is not the case. A study in the *Journal of Sports Medicine and Physical Fitness* showed that most men overestimate their calories burned after exercise. And well-known theories suggest that guys also underestimate the calories they consume. Stick to nutrient-dense foods post-workout to ensure you're maintaining the calorie deficit you're working toward.

Overeating can happen gradually as well as in the form of one massive cheat day. Maybe you've started attending a weekly happy hour. Or maybe you bought new dishware, and your portion sizes have increased without you realizing it. Of course, exactly what you're eating more of matters. Adding an extra portion of vegetables to your plate every day isn't a bad thing. But the processed stuff...that can add up. In a paper published in the *American Journal of Clinical Nutrition,* researchers found evidence that people who ate more refined grains—a category that includes white bread, white rice, muffins, bagels, pancakes, and the like—had more visceral fat. In contrast, people who ate whole grains—brown rice, oatmeal, popcorn, and grains like kasha and bulgur—had less visceral fat. This plan makes it easy to add more whole grains to your diet with simple recipes and swaps for refined carbs.

Your Alcohol Intake

It's no secret that alcohol = empty calories, and it will not help you lose weight. Light beers typically clock in around 100 calories, and your higher alcohol

025

THE LOSE YOUR GUT GUIDE

content craft beers can jump into the 300-calorie range. When you're out for the night, things can add up very quickly. Of course, the calories in alcohol alone aren't the only part that is detrimental to your waistline. There is also the tendency for booze to make us crave high-fat, greasy grub. The burger and

THE PERILS OF PROCESSED FOODS

On any diet, calories are king, and they can't be avoided. If you eat more than you burn, you will gain weight. This is known as a calorie surplus. But the types of foods you eat do make a difference to your metabolism, your ability to gain muscle, and your need to eat more or less food. Processed foods (like cakes and cookies) that are high in refined carbohydrates and sugars cause bursts in your blood glucose and raise your levels of insulin. This sends a chemical signal to your brain that makes you crave more food. As a result, you listen to your body's "need" (even if you're not really hungry) and continue to eat more at your current meal—and the next, say Syracuse University researchers.

fries at night. The bacon, egg, and cheese the next morning.

And then there is how your body actually handles drink after drink. Your body breaks down alcohol via various organs, including your stomach and pancreas, but your liver bears the burden of turning alcohol into less damaging forms. Through that process, the toxic byproducts from alcohol may lead to inflammation in your pancreas, which could potentially harm your insulin-producing cells and impair your fat metabolism. Stick to one or two drinks a day, and always down 'em with a healthy meal and proper hydration, says Abeyta.

Your Activity Level

Even little changes to your daily routine can decrease the calories you burn. Maybe you moved closer to a bus stop and have less of a walk on your morning commute. Maybe you started working from home and don't need to leave your couch during the day. Or perhaps you switched up your workout or cut out your warmup. These seemingly small actions accumulate over time. Even if you keep your diet completely the same,

CHAPTER 2 | **What Causes Belly Fat**

cutting out little bouts of movement can cause you to gain weight because all activities, laborious or not, require your body to burn some calories.

Your Sleep Routine

Ever spend the night tossing and turning then find yourself hovering over the snack table at work the following day, ALL day? There's actually a process occurring in your body when you're sleep deprived that makes you want to eat more. Your endocannabinoid (eCB) system plays a role in determining when you're hungry. When it gets out of whack, you might feel hungry even when you don't physically need food. A 2016 study in the journal *Sleep* looked at two groups of participants: one group that got 8.5 hours of sleep per night and another that got 4.5 hours per night. After the shorter night of sleep, the participants' eCB levels were higher and lasted longer in the afternoon than when they got 8.5 hours of rest. They also had stronger appetites. Clocking enough zzz's not only helps avoid this eCB mishap, but it also may help you lose the right kind of weight. In a small 2019 study published in *Annals of Internal Medicine*, volunteers on a reduced-calorie diet slept either 5.5 or 8.5 hours a night. In 2 weeks, they both lost a little more than 6.5 pounds—but those who slept more lost twice as much of that from fat.

Your Daily Schedule

Having a jam-packed calendar on its own won't cause you to gain weight, but if not managed properly, it can lead to a ton of poor health decisions that go straight to your gut. When you're booked morning, noon, and night every day, you likely don't have time to work out. Even if you manage to pencil in a sweat sesh, chances are you're so tightly wound from the rest of your demanding day that you can't give it your all. When life gets hectic, personal health is often the first thing to get cut from the grind. That might mean resorting to eating takeout several nights a week or pouring an extra nightcap to just chill out.

Your Takeout Habit

When dining out, people eat, on average, 190 more calories per meal than they do at home. The problem isn't just that some restaurant meals contain

THE LOSE YOUR GUT GUIDE

more calories than any of us should be eating in an entire day—although that's certainly part of it. It's also that we're hardwired to eat when we smell or see delicious food, and that hardwiring is nearly impossible to override with mere willpower. That's probably why dieters report feeling most tempted when in restaurants and least tempted when at home. "Yeah, yeah, yeah," you might be thinking, "I can splurge every once in a while. It's simple. I'll just eat less the following day. Problem solved." Maybe not, thanks to a phenomenon known as the "second meal effect." Leftover from our feast-or-famine days, this survival mechanism makes us feel hungrier after a high-calorie meal, and we need more food rather than less to feel satisfied. When you eat out, research shows, you're also more likely to eat saturated fat and sodium, which can torpedo your fat-loss goals. When you eat at home, on the other hand, you're more likely to consume fruits, vegetables, whole grains, and other foods that are good for your health as well as your waistline. To stay in the instant weight-loss zone, do just one simple thing: Eat at home. If that's not possible, use the tips on page 57 to dine out the smart way.

How Fat Happens

We're all born with the same number of fat cells (about 40 billion, give or take). As we grow up, the number of fat cells we have increases until after our pubescent and adolescent years, when they are pretty much set. In the past, it was assumed that the only difference between overweight people and thin ones was that overweight or obese people had all their fat cells filled to maximum capacity. It's now known that we can—and do, in fact—"grow" more fat cells in adulthood. This is because when fat cells expand to their maximum size, they divide and increase the number of fat cells. Some obese people have more fat cells than nonobese people. But in the end, both the number and the size of the fat cells determine the amount of fat someone has.

Why you can't lose your belly bulge is about way more than one simple decision, like a tendency to snack too much. Many of the weight-gain factors listed here are connected—and that's a good thing. When you tackle one, it can have a positive impact on another. For example, creating a little more breathing room in your schedule will help you make time for healthy meal prep and likely decrease your overall stress levels. In addition to these belly fat triggers, there are other, less common factors, like certain medications that can mess with your weight, particularly depression medications. Disorders that affect your endocrine system can also cause weight gain, although such conditions more often impact women than men. Whatever is causing your waistline to widen, addressing it is not only going to help your weight but your well-being in general. (Who was ever worse off for cutting stress out of their life?) The dangers of belly fat permeate so much more than just your clothing size. It's part of a cycle of unhealthy choices that can leave you at greater risk for disease and being generally unwell. When you get this one part of your body in check, you open the door for so many other good things.

PART 2

The secret to losing your gut once and for all isn't about one big change. It's about consistent small yet smart hacks to how you move, eat, and think. This is how you do it.

HOW TO
LOSE IT FOR GOOD

CHAPTER 3 | Maximize The Way You Move

Chapter 3

MAXIMIZE THE WAY YOU MOVE

You know belly fat can't be blasted with a single move. As great as it would be to only have to focus on crunches and planks to get the physique you want, the truth is you need a more well-rounded approach. Luckily, you don't have to memorize a complicated routine or spend hours on the treadmill to lose your gut. There is one strategy that can zap body fat all over faster than any other method and that can give you the maximum results with minimal effort.

You've probably always thought of working out to lose weight in two categories: You either head to the treadmill or make gains in the weight room. In the long-standing debate, cardio enthusiasts say you'll burn fat by torching calories when you increase heart rate. Weight lifters, however, believe excess fat is best shed by increasing muscle mass, because muscle burns more calories throughout the day.

While both statements are true, there's no one "right" exercise to transform your body. However, there are multiple ways to train smart so you can maximize your workouts and achieve results faster.

THE TRUTH ABOUT CARDIO

Cardiovascular exercise, of course, will

THE LOSE YOUR GUT GUIDE

use calories. It mostly hinges on blasting your heart rate in order to burn calories. The key is understanding how hard your heart should be working, and the best way to measure your effort is to find out the top end of your ticker's capacity: your estimated maximum heart rate (MHR).

You might have heard of the old-school method for calculating your heart rate max—220 minus your age. By that formula, if you're 25 years old, your max is 195 beats per minute (bpm). However, studies have shown that this formula is often inaccurate, especially the older you get.

Instead, multiply your age by 0.7 and subtract that from 208. This tends to be more accurate as you get older.

So, say you're 40 years old.

40 x 0.7 = 28
208 - 28 = 180 (Max Heart Rate)

To make training effective, you should aim to get your heart rate up to a certain level during exercise—and keep it there.

These ranges are commonly known as heart rate zones, and they have different potential benefits for your workout.

Three Main Heart Rate Zones

Aerobic/low intensity:
50–75 percent of MHR

Anaerobic/low intensity:
75–85 percent of MHR

Anaerobic/high intensity:
85+ percent of MHR

Contrary to what you may think, the optimal fat-burning zone is a relatively low intensity—specifically, 50 to 75 percent of MHR. "This is the zone where your body is primarily using fat as a fuel source rather than carbohydrates," says heart rate training expert Bryant Walrod, MD. "Once you creep above that 75 percent, your body starts using carbs."

Due to flawed logic, people often train too hard during their cardio bouts, hoping to burn fat quickly by pushing themselves as hard as possible. Since improving your body composition is the goal,

CHAPTER 3 | Maximize The Way You Move

try bringing the intensity down and increasing the length of workout time. Use a heart monitor to track your heart rate as you're working out. If you don't have one, you can also place your index and middle finger against your pulse. Count the number of beats in a 15-second span, and multiply that number by 4. By learning how easy or hard you're working, you can pace yourself to keep from fatiguing as well.

WHY YOU CAN'T SKIP STRENGTH TRAINING

While cardio can help with your belly fat goals, strength training helps build more muscle. The gains that come will indirectly help you lose belly fat, and you'll also be burning calories as you strength train too. How? Well, muscle is your metabolism—the more muscle you have, the more calories you burn at rest.

You might've heard about a long-standing myth that a pound of muscle burns 50 calories a day. By this logic, if you were to put on an extra 10 pounds of muscle, you would theoretically be burning an extra 500 calories a day at rest. Seems like a very compelling

justification for lifting more. However, recent studies have shown that a pound of muscle only really burns about 6 to 7 calories a day. The good news is that it's still three times more than what you burn with every pound of fat, and putting on muscle still revs up your metabolism.

How much you elevate your metabolism after your workout is directly related to the amount of muscle you activate at any one time. So, you'll want to focus on movements that work multiple muscles as opposed to those that attempt to isolate muscle groups. For instance, you'll experience a much greater boost in metabolism by performing 10 repetitions of a dumbbell row, which challenges biceps, lats, and abs at the same time, compared with 10 repetitions of an isolation exercise such as the biceps curl.

In addition, by training your whole body each session, you'll work the most muscle possible. A University of Wisconsin study found that when men performed a full-body workout involving just three big-muscle exercises—the bench press, power clean, and squat—their

CHAPTER 3 | **Maximize The Way You Move**

metabolisms were elevated for 39 hours afterward. What's more, they also burned a greater percentage of their calories from fat during this time, compared with men who didn't do a total-body workout. That's because strength training creates a level of muscle damage that increases metabolism postexercise during the recovery and repair process. But while it's good to have your body moving every day, workouts shouldn't take you to the point of fatigue and exhaustion. Complete an intense full-body weight workout 3 days a week, resting a day between sessions, and you'll keep your metabolism humming along in a much higher gear at all times.

As you build muscle, you'll reap other benefits too. For example, the more muscle you pack on, the more you'll help tighten and stabilize your joints. It might not sound thrilling, but sturdier joints decrease the chances you injure them. This is especially true for two of your largest ball-and-socket joints, the hip and the shoulder. Building muscle in the right places can help stabilize both joints, which often grow brittle with age and lack of use (which happens

frequently in today's desk job–driven culture). The longer you stay healthy and injury-free, the better equipped your body is to lift more, move more, and build more muscle, which inevitably help in burning away more fat. And if we're all being honest, your best ability is your availABILITY to continue your strength-training program, so do all you can to keep your body primed for movement.

THE MOST EFFECTIVE WORKOUT TO BLAST BELLY FAT

If you don't have the luxury of logging long hours at the gym, there is a way to reap the combined benefits of the fat-torching potential of cardio and the muscle-building power of strength-training: intervals.

Working out in intervals is a great way to maximize your calorie burn in a short amount of time by alternating between short bursts of intense effort and periods of lower intensity or rest. Greek researchers have found that performing intervals during your regular workout may help you lose more belly

035

THE LOSE YOUR GUT GUIDE

fat than steady-state cardio.

In the study, participants performed hour-long workouts four times a week. While everyone did 40 minutes of strength training, they were divided into two groups for cardio. One group ran for 20 minutes on treadmills, and the other group performed body-weight intervals for 20 minutes.

At the end of 8 weeks, the interval participants lost 2 inches of belly fat compared to the runners, who lost less than 1 inch. The researchers think interval training contributes to your body's afterburn effect.

The key in this really is intensity. The intensity resets your metabolism to a higher rate during your workout, so it takes hours for your body to cool down again. This is what's known as EPOC (excess postexercise oxygen consumption). That means you burn calories long after you've finished your workout compared to doing a workout at a continuous moderate pace, according to a 2017 study from the *European Journal of Applied Physiology*.

305

Calories a 240-pound guy burns walking slowly for an hour. Move like you're late for a meeting and the tally goes up to 469.

In another study, published in the *British Journal of Sports Medicine*, researchers crunched the data from 36 previous studies involving 1,012 people that compared the effects of interval training with continuous moderate-intensity exercise over at least 4 weeks' time.

Study authors split interval training into two categories: HIIT (high-intensity interval training) and sprint interval training. They defined HIIT as exercise that's done at 80 percent or more of your max heart rate and sprint interval training as exercise that's equal to or higher than your VO_2 max (this means going all out). While the protocols for each varied among the studies, the most widely used HIIT routine included 4 minutes of high-intensity work

036

CHAPTER 3 | Maximize The Way You Move

followed by 3 minutes of recovery. As for sprints, most used 30 seconds of "all-out" effort alternated with 4 minutes of recovery, or 8 seconds of work with 12 seconds of recovery.

Moderate-intensity exercise is defined as a continuous effort where you hit 55 to 70 percent of your max heart rate or 40 to 60 percent of your VO_2 max. Again, steady-state routines varied but ranged from 10 to 60 minutes, with those of 40 to 45 minutes and 29 to 35 minutes as the most common.

The findings? While people lost weight and body fat from both types of interval training (HIIT and sprint) and continuous moderate-intensity exercise, interval training as a whole was more effective. Those who did either kind of interval training lost about 29 percent more weight than those who did continuous moderate-intensity exercise.

While the research found that intervals are better for weight loss, it doesn't mean more intervals are even better. Because these workouts are more taxing on your body, you shouldn't do them as often as you do easy runs. Recovery time is also crucial in making sure your body continues to burn fat.

So how to put the research into practice? For best results with the Lose Your Gut meal plan, follow the workout program on page 127. When you need a change of pace, try the calorie-torching exercises in this section. Each will help you blast fat as is, but for a bigger burn we included easy ways to add intervals. If you choose to do intervals, do the exercise for 30 seconds every minute and rest for the remaining 30 seconds. As you progress, you can increase your time to 45 seconds of activity and 15 seconds of rest. Remember, you want to be working at your maximum—leaving you out of breath by the end of that interval.

Running
Whether you love it or hate it, running is one of the best and simplest ways to burn calories—and you don't need a treadmill to do it. Just lace up your shoes and hit the road.

A study published in the August 2018 issue of the *Journal of Clinical*

THE LOSE YOUR GUT GUIDE

Investigation Insight revealed that performing an endurance exercise at 70 percent of VO_2 max also increases the production of the hormone FGF21, which has a positive effect on metabolism. The higher your metabolism, the more calories you burn at rest. The good news is that running at 70 percent of VO_2 max isn't that difficult. It's just a little faster than your easy pace and a little slower than marathon pace.

Running in intervals—speeding up and slowing down your pace—will help make the minutes and miles go by quickly. Run in fartleks, which means speedplay in Swedish, where you pick up the pace every other street lamp or water hydrant you hit and then slow down after you pass the next one.

LEVEL UP!

Start out with a 5-minute jog. Then alternate between 10-second sprint intervals and 50-second moderately paced jogs. Use that jog to catch your breath, then hit the next sprint hard. Perform these intervals for 15 minutes, then end with a 5-minute jog. When you start to feel stronger in your runs, try upping the sprint effort to 20 seconds with 40 seconds of jogging.

Jump Rope

If you can't remember the last time you jumped rope, it's time to get back into the swing of things. The most basic piece of workout equipment gives you a full-body workout with a ton of fat-burning potential. Moderate-intensity rope jumping—about 100 to 120 skips per minute—burns about 13 calories a minute, according to the Compendium of Physical Activities.

Start off by perfecting your speed skipping form for short periods, 2 minutes at most. Keep your arms relatively still at

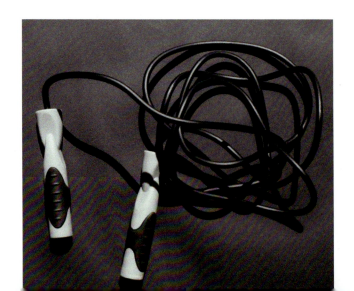

your sides, rotate your wrists to spin the rope, and jump off the ground only high enough so that you clear the rope. Land as softly as possible on the balls of your feet, ready to spring up again on the next rotation.

> **LEVEL UP!**

Start with 60 seconds of freestyle rope jumping. You can jump with two feet, one foot, alternate, skip, or twist your hips. Fire up your quads and glutes to help you explode from the ground, and engage your core to keep you upright and stable as you land. Have a blast with this one. Next, put down your rope and do 30 seconds of mountain climbers. Return for 60 seconds of freestyle rope jumping. End with 30 seconds in a plank. Rest for 2 minutes and repeat the cycle. Complete 3 rounds.

Strength Training

A recent study from North Dakota State University showed that you can burn 346 calories in just 13 minutes of a simple 6-exercise resistance circuit: bench press, bent-over row, biceps curl, lying triceps extension, leg extension, and lying leg curl. Higher-intensity total-body resistance training is better for burning calories because it increases both anaerobic and aerobic energy expenditures. This means that you burn calories both during and after your workout.

> **LEVEL UP!**

Pick up one dumbbell and complete 10 squats, 10 dumbbell rows per arm, and 10 of any push-up variation of your choice. Move right into the next exercise as you finish the reps. Do 3 rounds. Rest for 1–2 minutes between each round. As

THE LOSE YOUR GUT GUIDE

you get stronger, increase the weight of the dumbbell or use two.

Spinning

If you don't like running, spinning is a great alternative for burning calories and building endurance. It is a low-impact workout that'll crank up your heart rate. But there's more to pushing the pedal than speed. By practicing good form and engaging your core as well as your thighs and glutes, spinning can be a full-body workout.

Whether you're doing a heavy climb in first position or sprinting in second, your core is the key to spinning efficiently and quickly. And as you drive your foot down with each stroke, it's all about squeezing your inner thighs.

LEVEL UP!

Warm up on the bike for 10 minutes. Go as hard as you can for 30 seconds; pedal easily for 60 seconds. Repeat four times except after the fourth work interval, pedal easy for 4 minutes. Repeat the whole cycle 3 more times for a total of 37 minutes of exercise.

HIIT

HIIT workouts are, by far, one of the most effective ways to burn calories and hike your metabolism. They strengthen your muscles while spiking your heart rate. The best part is these workouts don't have to last very long. Some HIIT workouts can last for only 10 minutes, but the key is to push your body to its limits with all-out energy.

When you go all-out for short intervals, you quickly deplete your body's oxygen stores. This forces your body to work harder afterward to reestablish its oxygen bank. So, while you might burn as many calories during a jog, your body continues to burn more after the intervals.

Research has shown that HIIT workouts are super effective at burning belly fat, aka the worst kind of fat that puts you at risk for heart disease and other health conditions.

LEVEL UP!

The most efficient HIIT drill is the Tabata: 20-second intervals of maximum effort followed by 10-second rests for a

040

CHAPTER 3 | Maximize The Way You Move

total of 4 minutes. This 12-minute gear-free sweat fest is perfect when you're pinched for time: push-ups, alternating prisoner lunges, and mountain climbers, all for 4-minute Tabata drills each. Rest 2 minutes between each Tabata sequence.

Battle Ropes

Battle ropes are an excellent, no-fuss way to get a full-body strength training and cardio workout. In a recent College of New Jersey study comparing various workout styles, battle-rope exercises came in first in terms of total oxygen consumption and an average calorie burn of 10.3 calories per minute. Working at a high intensity, battle ropes not only increase your heart rate in seconds, but they're a great stress reliever too.

To use them properly: Hold one end of the rope with each hand, and stand with your feet shoulder-distance apart. Bend your knees slightly, and keep your chest up as you alternate whipping your arms to send waves down to the rope anchor. Experiment with different tempos and movement, whipping faster with one arm while slamming the rope hard with the other.

LEVEL UP!

Start with making alternating waves with each arm. For the next 5 minutes, try to maintain these waves. Don't worry about speed or intensity. Just try to endure. Try this for another 2 rounds. Rest 1 minute between rounds.

Swimming

If you're looking for a total-body cardio workout that's kind to your joints, swimming is it. Water adds an element of resistance, forcing you to recruit more muscles to move efficiently and use oxygen wisely, so it can be a total calorie-burner too.

Swimming at a somewhat casual pace—about 50 yards a minute—burns about 625 calories per hour. Kick that up to a high-level recreational athlete, where you're swimming 75 yards in a minute, and you'll burn a little more than 750 calories an hour. Churning out laps doesn't specifically burn belly fat, but if it's something that you'll do consistently because you enjoy it, it will help you drop pounds all over, including your belly.

3 Good Reasons to Vary Your Workout Routine

Finding the best workout that fits your lifestyle can be daunting, but remember that you don't need to stick to the same routine either. Changing it up often offers big benefits.

1. BATTLE BOREDOM: It's natural to get sick of the same spin class. Trying something new, like kickboxing or weight lifting, will feel less monotonous and improve your adherence.

2. PREVENT INJURIES: When you continually stress the same muscles—especially if you have bad form—you open yourself up to injuries. Changing your routine to work on different muscles on different days gives your body time to recover, making it more efficient at building strength and burning calories at the same time.

3. IMPROVE OVERALL HEALTH: Both cardio and strength have their virtues. Cardiovascular activities may help make your heart stronger, improve sleeping habits, reduce joint stiffness, and lower blood pressure and stress. Strength training increases bone density, lean muscle mass, and boosts your metabolism.

As with any exercise, the key to losing weight is to be consistent. Swim coaches talking with athletes who want to get stronger and faster encourage them to "swim less more often." You get more out of a swim when your technique is good, so getting in the water more frequently beats banging out a long session where you're just fighting falling-apart technique at the end.

Once your technique stays in place for a whole workout, see if you can make one swim a week slightly longer than the others. This will not only allow you to burn more calories, it will improve your endurance so you can swim stronger for longer in future sessions and gradually extend your time in the pool.

LEVEL UP!

To burn more calories in less time, break your workout into sets. Try swimming 4 laps at 70 percent, 4 at 80, and 4 at 90, resting between each set of 4. Then descend the ladder (4 at 90, 4 at 80, 4 at 70). The change in pace will also help keep you mentally engaged throughout your entire workout and break up the monotony of swimming lap after lap.

THE LOSE YOUR GUT GUIDE

How to Torch Calories When You Have No Time

While having a regular workout routine is optimal, it's not always the easiest habit to stick with when you're new to the gym or tied to an unpredictable schedule. Instead, you'll have to find ways to move more throughout the day. In fact, a little movement all day long may actually be beneficial to your waistline. A study from the University of Missouri found that active nonexercisers burned more calories than people who ran 35 miles a week but were otherwise sedentary. Bottom line: always take the path of more movement. Here are 20 ways to do just that.

▶ Opt to take the stairs instead of the elevator.

▶ Park the car farther away from the grocery store.

▶ Set reminders to get up from your desk every hour or so.

▶ Take a walk at lunch.

▶ Clean your house (all that reaching and bending adds up).

▶ Drink more water. More water = getting up to stretch your legs during refills and bathroom breaks.

▶ Walk while you text. But maybe only indoors and away from other people.

▶ Work out while watching TV. Even just some crunches.

▶ Or get up during the ads.

▶ Try a new commute, like biking, if you're close enough to the office.

▶ Do some calf raises while you brush your teeth.

▶ Plan your next hangout around movement, like walking around a park or museum.

▶ Blast your favorite song and move like you're front row at a show.

▶ Shop in person. You'll move more than by simply clicking "add to cart."

▶ Schedule walking meetings if you can.

▶ Shop at a farmers' market and BYO bags.

▶ Have more sex!

▶ Do some yard work.

▶ At a party? Stand instead of nabbing a spot on the couch.

▶ Take a walk to your favorite restaurant.

Moving continuously throughout the day helps your body burn calories 24/7—not just when you're in the gym. These little tweaks can make all the difference, so try adding a few to your day-to-day routine, and build onto your routine from there.

Chapter 4

FUEL YOUR BODY FOR FAT BURNING

Food is often the most confusing part of the weight-loss equation. Your eating patterns are most likely ingrained in your routine from hundreds of days spent doing the same thing. Maybe it's grabbing a snack at 3 p.m. every day. Or a huge breakfast every Saturday. Most diets completely overhaul

045

THE LOSE YOUR GUT GUIDE

your way of being by cutting carbs or requiring elaborate daily calculations. Luckily, the secret to blasting through belly fat with food boils down to three simple principles:

1. Stay in a moderate calorie deficit.
2. Hit your optimal protein intake.
3. Eat a high volume of fruits and vegetables.

Abeyta developed the meal plan and recipes in this guide to hit these goals. The calorie counting and protein tallying and plate balancing are done for you. If you follow the menu, you will spend the next 3 weeks feeling full and

MACROS VS. MICROS

Your body requires a diverse mix of nutrients to keep the engine humming. Those you need in large quantities are macronutrients. They consist of protein, carbohydrate, and fat. Those you need in small quantities are micronutrients, like iron, calcium, magnesium, and vitamin D.

energized while you burn through fat. Simple as that. Technically, you could skip right to the plan and start chowing down, but understanding the "why" behind this program will help keep your head in the game even when cheat-day temptations come knocking at your door. Refer back to these pages when you start to falter, and we promise you'll come back with a clear focus.

DON'T OVERLOOK CALORIES

For decades now, dieting has become overly complicated. There have been eating plans targeting your fat intake, your carb intake, your fiber intake. Maybe you've tried some of these diets and ditched them somewhere down the line. That's normal...maybe even expected. When bombarded with too much information, too many rules, we are liable to lose track of the guidelines and just give up. That's why we've boiled belly fat loss down to just the three principles in this chapter. It's so easy, you don't even have to think about it.

Now, it is true that your body relies on a wide range of nutrients to carry out

CHAPTER 4 | Fuel Your Body For Fat Burning

essential processes, including burning fat, so you can't completely ignore those little numbers on the nutrition label like fiber and fat. But introducing all these different factors really clouds the truth around how your body loses fat, which is by burning more calories than you consume. The beauty of a moderate calorie deficit approach, like the one in this plan, is that it helps you hit all the right micro- and macronutrient goals without even really trying, as long as you focus on the right types of foods. Bottom line: You need to eat more of the right calories in order to survive on fewer calories.

It helps to have a little primer on calories. A calorie is a unit of energy. For your body to do anything—circulate blood, take in oxygen, move muscles—it requires energy. It gets this energy from fat, protein, and carbs, all of which contain calories. One gram of fat has 9 calories, while 1 gram of carbs and 1 gram of protein each has 4 calories. When your body has more energy, or calories, than it needs, it saves it for later (calorie surplus). And it tends to save it as fat. Side note: Alcohol contains 7 calories per gram (save that one for your next trivia night).

So, in order to lose weight, you need to make sure you are using up all the calories you are consuming and then some. When your body needs more calories than you supplied it with, it taps into stored glycogen (the stored form of carbs) for energy. If this calorie deficit continues over a sustained period, it will begin to metabolize fat (where you've been storing all those excess calories).

So, why go for just a moderate calorie deficit when you could slash your intake to a fraction of what it normally is? First, and most importantly, it's sustainable. Highly restrictive diets seldom stick. Although you might be able to live off protein bars and weight-loss shakes for a brief period, the drastic shift in your eating patterns will most likely cause you to binge it all back at some point. After a massive cheat day or week, you might feel ready to jump back in, but the cycle will likely continue, and any downward movement on the scale will be fleeting. In addition to being just plain hard to maintain, major calorie deficits also

047

THE LOSE YOUR GUT GUIDE

rarely work because they are unhealthy. Because you aren't eating a lot, you're probably not getting a wide variety of nutrients, the things you need just to keep going. You'll likely feel sluggish, sleepy, and unmotivated—not the best mode for weight loss. Ultimately, your body needs a significant portion of calories just to keep churning through the day. You need to give it that in order to be a functioning human embarking on a full-on weight-loss journey.

REMEMBER: PROTEIN IS YOUR FAT-BURNING SECRET

Protein is vital to life. It is typically branded as the holy grail nutrient for anyone looking to bulk up because it's made from amino acids that are essential for building and maintaining muscles and bones. It also helps regulate a host of cellular processes affecting everything from your immune function to the transportation of oxygen through the bloodstream. But one of its most potent powers is its ability to help you get lean. This mighty macronutrient is unbeatable when it comes to squashing hunger. Researchers have found that

Q: How many calories do you burn a day?

A: *The answer is totally unique to your body and lifestyle. Your daily burn is known as your personal energy expenditure. Part of this number is determined by the physical activity you do in a day. The other part is influenced by your resting energy expenditure (REE), or how efficiently your body burns calories at rest. Your REE is dependent on three factors, all of which are somewhat variable but may shift throughout your lifespan based on lean body mass, level of physical activity, change in weight overall, or metabolic state. They are:*

1. BASAL METABOLIC RATE: the number of calories your body requires to perform its most basic functions, from breathing to sleeping.

2. PHYSICAL ACTIVITY ENERGY EXPENDITURE: physical activity throughout the days and weeks.

3. THERMIC EFFECT OF FOOD: the calories your body uses to digest a meal.

CHAPTER 4 | **Fuel Your Body For Fat Burning**

consuming protein stimulates the release of satiety signals in the small intestine, helping you to feel full and to fight off the urge to snack your way through the day. Load up on protein-rich foods at mealtime, and you'll no longer be at the mercy of midmorning stomach pangs. Aim for at least 20 grams of protein per meal.

Of course, anyone who has ever stared into the deep, dark abyss of their fridge at 11 p.m. knows that eating isn't just about feeling hungry. It is very possible to be Thanksgiving-level stuffed and still decide to try every single dessert on the table. Cravings are very, very real. Protein actually makes them go away. Brain scans indicate that consumption of protein decreases activity in regions of the brain that stimulate cravings. So, not only will a helping of, say, protein-packed salmon leave you feeling full and energized, it will also take your mind off whatever junk is hiding in your pantry.

And in case you need another reason to get behind protein, research has even suggested that it can boost your total calorie burn. A British study found that participants who increased the percentage of protein-based calories in their diets burned 71 more calories a day (that's 7.4 pounds a year) than those on low-protein diets. Your body uses more energy to digest protein than refined carbs, for example, so the basic act of eating it helps you burn calories.

WHEN IN DOUBT, PICK PRODUCE

Fruits and vegetables are always part of the answer when it comes to losing weight, partly because scientists have yet to learn of anyone packing on pounds from eating too much kale. Produce packs a major nutritional punch with very few calories. Ever look at the nutrition label on a bag of spinach? You could eat the entire bag and not break 100 calories. What you would get is high levels of vitamins K and A, as well as manganese, folate, magnesium, iron, copper, vitamin B2, vitamin B6, vitamin E, calcium, potassium, and vitamin C. It's the same story with every piece of produce you find at the grocery store. Tons of nutrients, very few calories. Being low in calories means you can pile

049

CHAPTER 4 | **Fuel Your Body For Fat Burning**

these foods high on your plate, no counting necessary. (And who doesn't love having something you can relentlessly stack on your fork when it comes to dieting?)

The nutrients in fruits and vegetables

STAY HYDRATED

All of your body's chemical reactions, including your metabolism, depend on water. If you are dehydrated, you may be burning up to 2 percent fewer calories, according to researchers at the University of Utah who monitored the metabolic rates of 10 adults as they drank varying amounts of water per day. In the study, those who drank either eight or twelve 8-ounce glasses of water a day had higher metabolic rates than those who had four.

Also, try drinking tap or mineral water. In a Swiss study, purified water didn't boost men's metabolic activity, but water that contained minerals did. Remember to drink from a smaller cup—the walk to get a refill will boost your workday activity!

---

help your body carry out its daily functions effortlessly. When your vital functions are taken care of, your body can focus on other tasks, like burning fat. Some fruits and vegetables actually aid in the fat-burning process. The amino acid arginine, which is abundant in watermelon, has been linked to weight loss, according to a study in the *Journal of Nutrition*. Researchers supplemented the diets of obese mice with arginine over 3 months and found that it decreased body-fat gains by a whopping 64 percent. Adding this amino acid to the diet enhanced oxidation of fat and glucose and increased lean muscle, which burns more calories than fat does. Most fruits and veggies will also help you feel fuller because they're a natural source of fiber. It takes a while for your body to digest fiber, so you likely won't feel the need to open the fridge again for some time if you pair your produce with other hunger-fighting ingredients, like Abeyta's done in this meal plan.

Once you hit your goal of losing belly fat, staying in shape will be a constant balancing act, but don't stress—the more you learn, the easier it'll get.

Chapter 5

GET YOUR MIND-SET RIGHT

You can read all the weight-loss books in the world, follow all the fit-fluencer accounts on social media, and buy every clean-eating ingredient at the grocery store, but your state of mind is the only thing that is going to get you to use the tools you're equipped with. It might be the reason you haven't been able to shed extra pounds in the past. You knew what you needed to do, but your mind waved the white flag while your body was still ready to forge onward.

CHAPTER 5 | Get Your Mind-Set Right

Change your mind and you will be un-stoppable. How? Work through these questions Abeyta uses to help clients start their weight-loss journey on the right foot.

WHY ARE YOU READING THIS BOOK?

Write down five reasons. And while you're at it, write this down: When your WHY is STRONG, the HOW appears. "Asking about your five whys is super simple and extremely powerful," says Abeyta. "It gets to the underlying cause of whatever you are facing. " Why five? In the first two to three answers to this question, you will likely jot down a conscious answer—something that you have likely rationalized for years or maybe even decades, says Abeyta. For example, you might be thinking about why you want to lose body fat. Your first two "whys" could be because you want to live a healthier life. As you go further, you then tap into reasons why you want to be healthier—maybe it's for your kids or to be more intimate with your partner again or to finally feel confident enough to go for that job promotion. You'll see that once you peel

the onion, you can then go deeper. Once you go deeper into the fourth and fifth questions, you get to the real reasons and the light bulb goes off.

IF YOUR MAIN OBSTACLE DIDN'T EXIST, HOW WOULD YOUR LIFE LOOK?

This powerful question allows you to overcome whatever obstacle is keeping you from this really important goal, says Abeyta. "Oftentimes we can create stories in our head about why a goal is unattainable. 'I don't have time,' 'Healthy foods are too expensive,' and 'I always quit, why would this be any different?' " he says. "Recognizing the stories that you tell yourself can allow you to engage in the possibility of overcoming those same obstacles." And while this is not an easy task, speaking aloud how your weight-loss journey would feel without that challenge or barrier will allow your brain to bridge the gap so that it can open you up to find a solution.

WHAT ARE YOU DOING TO *NOT* ACHIEVE YOUR GOAL?

Abeyta says most of the time, his clients will come to him with massive goals that

053

THE LOSE YOUR GUT GUIDE

they have yet to achieve even though they have had them for many years and sometimes decades. So, he asks them this question: "In what ways are you sabotaging yourself to not achieve this goal that is so important to you?" The question is valuable because it helps them (and you) recognize that they're making choices every single day that will determine whether their success comes to them. Here are the answers Abeyta hears most often and how to address them:

Caving to cravings

Most of the time, people will often give in to cravings because they don't understand the role of emotional hunger and physical hunger. Sometimes your emotional need to eat might be that in the past, you weren't eating enough; but with this plan, you will be given guidance with how to eat and also why you eat.

Not moving enough

Working out is really important; however, your ability to remain active outside of exercise is going to be huge. Figure out a way to get in more steps, do more yardwork, or even get a standing desk to boost time spent on your feet.

Sweating the small stuff

Your stress is killing you. Work to manage your stress by emphasizing really great sleep hygiene, that is, all the little things you do before and during bed. Try getting to bed at the same time each night, and work to get 7 to 8 hours of rest before starting the day. This by itself will allow you enough rest to combat ongoing stress and what comes from that.

Eating on autopilot

Your eating behavior will be imperfect, so your ability to work in mindful eating tactics will be huge. Try getting to a point where you are able to arrive at your meal comfortably hungry, and work to leave your meal at 80 percent full. This will do wonders.

Keep your answers to these questions somewhere you can easily access. It sounds simple, but just glancing at your list of reasons can help redirect you from 3 hours of snacking on the couch to a night of healthy choices.

THE TOOLS

PART 3

Consider these your secret weapons to building a better body. Here, we break down exactly how to eat, move, and think your way to a leaner physique. Follow along and see results in no time.

Chapter 6

THE MEAL PLAN

Abeyta designed this meal plan to keep you full, pack in a ton of flavor, and help you lose those extra pounds around your middle once and for all. But he also created it to be extremely easy. Making healthy grub doesn't have to be complicated. For every day of the next 21 days, you'll see exactly what to eat, how much of it to eat, when to eat it, and how to prep it so you can enjoy eating it without worrying about a disaster in the kitchen. Everything you need to know is on the following pages, including shopping lists of everything you need to get at the

CHAPTER 6 | The Meal Plan

grocery store and a nutritional breakdown of every day. Abeyta also included leftovers and smart ways to use up ingredients on hand so you can minimize your time spent cooking. You can jump into the plan as is, but check out these tips for modifying and customizing for your lifestyle.

HOW MUCH CAN I EAT?

Unless otherwise noted, eat 1 serving of each meal or snack. Some recipes will require you to make multiple servings so you can save leftovers and eat them on another day, as indicated in the plan. The plan is designed to crush hunger all day with filling protein and fiber, but if you find your stomach growling, add extra veggies and fruit to your plate.

HOW CAN I MAKE MEAL PREP BEARABLE?

You don't have to spend hours on Sunday getting meals ready for the week—as long as you have these crucial kitchen tools on hand.

Essential Equipment
- Sharp knives: chef's, paring, and serrated
- Variously sized pots, saucepans, and skillets with lids
- Baking sheets and baking pans
- Food processor or blender
- Measuring cups
- Measuring spoons
- Steamer
- Grater
- Citrus juicer
- Cutting boards
- Cooking utensils: wooden spoons, flat spatula, rubber spatula, whisk, tongs
- Storage containers for leftovers and make-aheads

HOW CAN I EAT OUT AND STILL LOSE WEIGHT?

Going out to eat is about more than the grub—it serves up a change of scenery, social atmosphere, and sense of reward in addition to cooking you may never be able to replicate. Stick with the plan as laid out, then once you get to your desired weight, use these tips for eating out without ruining your progress.

Choose your meal at home, when you are not hungry. Check to see if the restaurant has an online menu, complete with nutrition information.

057

THE LOSE YOUR GUT GUIDE

Grilled dishes, salads, and veggie sides will probably be your best bets. If all of the meals are loaded with calories (they probably will be), plan to eat only half. Ask the server to wrap the other half before it ever hits the table.

Order first. That way you won't feel tempted when you hear your dining companion order the burger and fries followed by the molten chocolate cake.

Order ½ for here and the other ½ for take-home. This will help you navigate portioning and provide you with a chance toward mindful eating. Work this out; you got this!

Start with veggies. Your stomach doesn't count calories, but what it does count is volume. Eating high-volume vegetables can help your body sense an appropriate amount of fullness. Doing this will be tremendously helpful in any eating environment you are in.

Save alcohol for the meal—or even after the meal. That way it won't undo your inhibitions and trigger you to order or eat more than you planned.

HOW CAN I ALTER THE PLAN?

This plan is built to help you execute a moderate calorie deficit that will aid in your fat-loss journey. This can be done with a proper amount of exercise, non-exercise activity (walking, doing dishes, etc.), as well as quality sleep. However, from a food standpoint, this is how you can make sure to get the best from this meal plan:

Increase your veggie consumption. This will help you eat less over time.

Sip on water throughout your meal to help your body navigate its own fullness cues.

Work on stopping at 80 percent full for one or two meals out of the day. This will help your body sense fullness for longevity vs. eating everything all at once in 10 minutes.

Set a timer for 25 minutes, and aim to finish in that amount of time. Chances are you'll leave a couple bites.

CHAPTER 6 | The Meal Plan

CAN I SWAP OUT INGREDIENTS?

Absolutely! Here are some ways you can swap out ingredients in case you don't have them or you have some minor food aversions:

Vegetarian? Feel free to add modifications that allow your protein intake to stay up to par. Most days of this plan will give you close to 110 to 130 grams. Try working in high protein–containing plant foods like tempeh, tofu, beans, and legumes, all of which could provide close to 15 grams per 1 cup serving.

Vegan? Consider the aforementioned on top of supplementing a vegan-based protein powder for snacks while getting the necessary supplementation needed. You might need an extra boost of things like branched-chain amino acids (BCAAs), omega-3s, B12, vitamin D, and iodine.

Gluten-free? Substitute gluten ingredients in these recipes with a gluten-free alternative, like gluten-free bread or quinoa.

Dairy-free? You may want to consider substituting nondairy cheese, yogurts, and milks. Pretty much all varieties work well here — coconut, almond, oat, you name it.

CAN I DRINK ALCOHOL ON THIS PLAN?

You sure can! However, a good way to think about it is that alcohol is a socially permitted muscle diminisher, and your consumption absolutely matters. Per CDC guidelines, the maximum safe intake for men is 14 drinks per week. Of course, this could be seen as safe, but as it pertains to your ability to recover from your workouts, emphasize sleep, and maintain a calorie deficit, a nightly happy hour could be going against your overall fat-loss goals. Pure alcohol contains roughly 7 calories per gram. For reference, carbohydrates and protein both contain about 4 calories per gram, while fat contains about 9 calories per gram. This means that alcohol is nearly twice the calories as carbohydrates or protein and only slightly lower than fat. Work to drink responsibly, and consider substituting one of your snacks should you go out for a night of moderate drink-

THE LOSE YOUR GUT GUIDE

ing, i.e., 2 drinks during an outing.

HOW CAN I IMPROVE THIS PLAN EVEN MORE?

One of the greatest tools you can learn is to navigate mindful eating techniques. One of those is to get to a point where you are approaching meals with minimal hunger (not hangry) and working to leave your meals at 80 percent full. Here's a rating system that you can use to check in with your hunger and your fullness. Try to stay between a rating of 4 to 8:

0 Starving and beyond.
1 You are so hungry that you want to eat everything on the menu.
2 Everything on the menu begins to look good. You may be preoccupied with hunger.
3 You are hungry, and the urge to eat is strong.
4 A little hungry. You can wait to eat (1 hr.), but you know that you will be hungrier soon.
5 Neutral: not hungry, not full.
6 No longer hungry. You sense food in your belly, but you could definitely eat more.

7 Hunger is definitely gone. Stop here, and you may not feel hungry again for 3–4 hrs.
8 Not uncomfortable but definitely sense of fullness.
9 Moving into uncomfortable.
10 Very uncomfortable, maybe even painful.

WHAT DO I DO WHEN I FINISH THE MEAL PLAN?

Your body is not meant to be on a calorie deficit for life. In fact, most studies have shown that a calorie deficit shouldn't last more than 12 weeks without going into a short maintenance period and then reestablishing your deficit to lose the last couple of pounds. Stick with the plan for 12 weeks, then bump up your calorie intake in a healthy way with things like whole grains, healthy fats, fruits, and veggies.

CHAPTER 6 | The Meal Plan

PANTRY STAPLES

Make sure you have these essential items on hand before starting the meal plan.

1 small bottle **avocado oil**
1 small container **baking powder**
1 small container **black pepper**
1 small container **cayenne**
1 small container **chili powder**
1 small container **cinnamon**
1 small container **cocoa powder**
1 small jar **coconut oil**
1 container **cooking spray**
1 small container **cumin**
1 small container **ground ginger**
1 jar **honey**
1 bottle **maple syrup**
1 small bottle **mustard**
1 bottle **extra virgin olive oil**
1 small container **oregano**
1 small container **paprika**
1 small container **smoked paprika**
1 small container **pumpkin pie spice**
1 small container **salt**
1 small container **sea salt**
1 small bottle **sesame oil**
1 small bottle **tamari**
1 small container **dried thyme**
1 small container **turmeric**
1 small container **vanilla extract**
1 small bottle **apple cider vinegar**
1 small bottle **balsamic vinegar**
1 small bottle **red wine vinegar**

061

THE LOSE YOUR GUT GUIDE

WEEK

1

SHOPPING LIST

WEEK 1

Meats & Proteins

8 oz **beef**
6 oz **chicken**
1 lb **skinless, boneless chicken breast**
1 **cod filet**
1 dozen **eggs**
1 pint **egg whites**
1 (10-oz) container **hummus**
1 small container **chocolate protein powder**
1 small container **vanilla protein powder**
4 oz **sausage**
2 lb **shrimp**
1 (8-oz) block **firm tofu**
3½ oz sliced **turkey breast**

Dairy

1 quart **unsweetened almond milk**
1 block **cheddar cheese**
2 (32-oz) containers **plain Greek yogurt**

Produce

1 bunch **asparagus**
2 **avocados**
13 **bananas**
1 **bell pepper** of your choosing
1 **green bell pepper**

2 **red bell peppers**
2 large **yellow bell peppers**
2 (16-oz) bags **frozen berries**
1 pint **blueberries**
1 small bag **carrots**
1 **cauliflower**
1 bunch **celery**
1 bunch **cilantro**
2 ears **corn** (fresh, canned, or frozen)
2 **cucumbers**
1 head **garlic**
1 (1-inch) piece **ginger**
1 bunch **kale**
2 **kiwis**
1 head **lettuce**
1 **lime**
1 **onion**
1 bunch **green onion**
1 **red onion**
1 bunch **parsley**
3 **pears**
1 head **romaine leaves**
2 (6-oz) bags **baby spinach**
1 **tomato**
1 pint **cherry tomatoes**
2 large **zucchini**

Pantry

1 small package **slivered almonds**
1 (15.5-oz) can **black beans**
1 (15.5-oz) can **black beans** (or beans of your choosing)
1 quart **organic vegetable or chicken broth**
1 small container **cajun seasoning**
1 small package **chia seeds**
1 small bottle **coconut aminos**
1 small package **whole-grain crackers**
1 small package **ground flax seed**
1 bottle **lemon juice**
1 small container **oats**
1 (15-oz) can **pumpkin puree**
1 small package **pumpkin seeds**
1 small package **quinoa**
1 small package **raisins**
2 small containers **sesame seeds**
1 small container **tahini**
1 (15-oz) can **diced tomatoes or 1 large tomato**
1 (15-oz) can **fire-roasted diced tomatoes**
1 package **corn tortillas**
1 package **whole-wheat tortillas**

WEEK 1 MEAL PREP

DAY BEFORE STARTING

For Yogurt & Berries: Fill 2 airtight containers with 1 cup plain Greek yogurt and 1 cup frozen berries each.

For Hummus & Veggies Snack Box: Fill an airtight container with ½ red bell pepper, sliced, 2 stalks celery cut into small pieces, ⅓ cup blueberries, and ¼ cup hummus.

For Deli Snack Box: Hard-boil 1 egg.

ON DAY 3

For Yogurt with Pears: Fill 2 airtight containers with 1 cup plain Greek yogurt and 1¼ pears, sliced, each.

For Cinnamon Raisin Protein Cookies: Make cookies and store in airtight container.

063

THE LOSE YOUR GUT GUIDE

Week 1
DAY 1

BREAKFAST
Overnight Blueberry Oat Success (p. 82)
Refrigerate remaining in an airtight container for Day 3 breakfast.

`MEAL PREPPED`

SNACK
Yogurt & Berries
Top 1 cup plain Greek yogurt with 1 cup frozen berries (thawed).

LUNCH
Spicy Quinoa Tacos (p. 80)

DINNER
Garlicky Beef, Greens, and Quinoa
In a medium pan, cook 8 oz beef. Transfer to a bowl and set aside. To the same pan, add handful kale and season with a pinch of salt, 1 Tbsp coconut aminos, diced clove of garlic, pinch of ginger, and ½ stalk green onion. Cook until kale is tender, then set aside. Cook ¼ cup quinoa according to package directions. Makes 2 servings. Refrigerate leftovers in an airtight container for Day 2 lunch.

SNACK
Berry & Greek Yogurt Smoothie
To a blender, add 1 cup plain Greek yogurt, 2 Tbsp honey, 2 frozen bananas, 1 cup frozen berries, 2 Tbsp ground flax seed, and 2 cups water. Blend until smooth. Makes 2 servings. Refrigerate leftovers in an airtight container for Day 2 breakfast.

Nutrition (per Day): 1,930 calories, 102 g protein, 253 g carbohydrates (50 g fiber), 64 g fat

CHAPTER 6 | The Meal Plan

DAY 2

LEFTOVERS
BREAKFAST
Berry & Greek Yogurt Smoothie

SNACK
Hummus & Veggies Snack Box
Eat ½ red bell pepper, sliced, 2 stalks celery cut into small pieces, ⅓ cup blueberries, and ¼ cup hummus.

LEFTOVERS
LUNCH
Garlicky Beef, Greens, and Quinoa

DINNER
Anti-Inflammatory Chicken Salad (p. 91)
Refrigerate remaining in an airtight container for Day 3 lunch.

SNACK
Banana Cinnamon Smoothie
To a blender, add ½ cup vanilla protein powder, 2 Tbsp ground flax seed, 2 Tbsp chia seeds, 2 frozen bananas, 4 ice cubes, 2 cups water, and ½ tsp cinnamon. Blend until smooth. Makes 1 serving.

Nutrition (per Day): 1,610 calories, 128 g protein, 168 g carbohydrates (33 g fiber), 52 g fat

DAY 3

LEFTOVERS
BREAKFAST
Overnight Blueberry Oat Success

SNACK
Deli Snack Box
Eat ¼ cup pumpkin seeds, 5 whole-grain crackers, ½ cup cherry tomatoes, 1 oz cubed cheddar cheese, 1 hard-boiled egg, and 3½ oz rolled-up sliced turkey breast.

LEFTOVERS
LUNCH
Anti-Inflammatory Chicken Salad

DINNER
Roasted Cauliflower Burrito Bowl
Preheat the oven to 425°F. In a medium bowl, toss ¼ head of cauliflower, cut into florets, with pinch of cumin, chili powder, smoked paprika, and sea salt. Roast on a baking tray for 25 minutes, flipping halfway. Meanwhile, in a saucepan over medium-low, add ⅓ cup canned black beans (or beans of choice). Mash with the back of a spoon and simmer until warm. In a small bowl, mash ¼ avocado, ¼ clove minced garlic, and squeeze of lime juice to make guacamole. Serve cauliflower in a bowl topped with beans, guacamole, and cilantro, if desired. Makes 1 serving.

MEAL PREPPED
SNACK
Yogurt & Berries
Top 1 cup plain Greek yogurt with 1 cup frozen berries (thawed).

Nutrition (per Day): 1,935 calories, 138 g protein, 156 g carbohydrates (36 g fiber), 89 g fat

065

THE LOSE YOUR GUT GUIDE

DAY 4

BREAKFAST
Protein Breakfast Power Bowl (p. 85)

SNACK
Berry & Greek Yogurt Smoothie
To a blender, add 1 cup plain Greek yogurt, 2 Tbsp honey, 2 frozen bananas, 1 cup frozen berries, 2 Tbsp ground flax seed, and 2 cups water. Blend until smooth. Makes 2 servings. Refrigerate leftovers in an airtight container for Day 5 snack.

LUNCH
Hummus Veggie Wrap and Sliced Cucumber
Spread ¼ cup hummus on a whole-wheat tortilla and top with handful romaine leaves, ¼ avocado, ¼ cucumber, and ¼ bell pepper. Fold in the ends of the tortilla and roll tightly. Eat the rest of the cucumber slices as a side.

DINNER
Shrimp Zoodle Stir-Fry (p. 92)
Refrigerate remaining in an airtight container for Day 5 lunch.

MEAL PREPPED

SNACK
Yogurt with Pears
Top 1 cup plain Greek yogurt with 1¼ pears, sliced.

Nutrition (per Day): 1,829 calories, 111 g protein, 204 g carbohydrates (47 g fiber), 73 g fat

DAY 5

LEFTOVERS

BREAKFAST
Overnight Blueberry Oat Success

LEFTOVERS

SNACK
Berry & Greek Yogurt Smoothie

LEFTOVERS

LUNCH
Shrimp Zoodle Stir-Fry

SNACK
Kiwi Green Smoothie
To a blender, add 2 peeled kiwis, 1 frozen banana, ½ cup vanilla protein powder, 2 Tbsp chia seeds, 2½ cups baby spinach, 2 cups water, and 4 ice cubes. Blend until smooth.

DINNER
Lemon Cilantro Cod with Peppers
To a resealable food storage bag, add 1 Tbsp lemon juice, 3 Tbsp olive oil, ¾ cup cilantro, pinch of sea salt, and 1 cod filet. Massage bag to cover the cod in the mixture, then let sit in the fridge for 30 minutes. Heat the oven to 375°F. Coat a medium skillet with cooking spray and heat over medium. Add ¼ red bell pepper, ¼ yellow bell pepper, and ½ tomato, diced, and sauté for 8 to 10 minutes. Place cod fillets in baking dish, add cooked veggies, and cover with foil. Bake for 18 to 20 minutes or until fish flakes easily.

Nutrition (per Day): 1,783 calories, 134 g protein, 175 g carbohydrate (38 g fiber), 69 g fat

066

CHAPTER 6 | The Meal Plan

DAY 6

BREAKFAST
Chocolate Protein Pancakes (p. 88)
Refrigerate remaining in an airtight container for Day 9 and 11 breakfast.

SNACK
Cinnamon Raisin Protein Cookies
Preheat the oven to 350°F and line a baking sheet with parchment paper. In a medium bowl, mash ¾ ripe banana, then mix in 3 Tbsp egg whites and 1 Tbsp tahini. Add ¼ cup vanilla protein powder, ¼ cup dry oats, 2 Tbsp raisins, and 2 Tbsp ground flax, and mix well. Scoop batter onto baking sheet and bake for 18 to 22 minutes until golden brown. Makes 2 servings (2-3 cookies per serving). Store remaining in airtight container for today's afternoon snack.

LUNCH
Easy Chicken Fajitas
In a medium skillet, heat 1½ tsp olive oil. Add 3½ oz chicken, sliced into strips, chili powder, cumin, and salt to taste. Cook for 8 to 10 minutes, then add ¼ green, yellow, and red bell pepper, and onion and stir to coat. Cook for 5 minutes or until peppers are tender. Divide chicken and peppers between 2 corn tortillas. Makes 1 serving.

LEFTOVERS
SNACK Cinnamon Raisin Protein Cookies

DINNER
Paleo Grits with Shrimp & Sausage
Steam ½ head of cauliflower. Bring to a boil for 10 to 15 minutes and set aside. Add 4 oz shrimp, 4 oz sausage, and add cajun seasoning. Cook for 6 to 8 minutes in a separate medium-size pan. Transfer steamed cauliflower to a cutting board, chop finely, divide into bowls, and top with shrimp, sausage, and green onion (optional). Makes 2 servings. Refrigerate remaining in an airtight container for Day 7 breakfast.

SNACK
Pumpkin Pie Protein Smoothie
To a blender, add 2 cups almond milk, 1 cup pumpkin puree, 2 frozen bananas, pinch of pumpkin spice, ½ cup vanilla protein powder. Blend until smooth. Makes 2 servings. Refrigerate remaining in an airtight container for Day 7 snack.

Nutrition (per Day): 1,795 calories, 137 g protein, 174 g carbohydrates (29 g fiber), 65 g fat

DAY 7

LEFTOVERS

BREAKFAST
Paleo Grits with Shrimp & Sausage

LEFTOVERS

SNACK
Pumpkin Pie Protein Smoothie

LUNCH
Chicken, Lettuce, and Tomato Egg Wrap with Sweet Potato Hash Browns
In a mixing bowl, whisk 2 eggs. Coat a medium skillet with olive oil and heat over medium. Add ½ of the whisked egg, tilting pan in a circular motion to distribute egg evenly. Cook for 60 to 90 seconds then flip it and cook for 30 to 60 more. Repeat with remaining egg. Transfer 1 cooked egg to a plate and layer with lettuce, sliced tomato, and 2 oz cooked chicken. Top with the other egg and fold together to eat.

SNACK
Cinnamon Raisin Protein Cookies
Preheat the oven to 350°F and line a baking sheet with parchment paper. In a medium bowl, mash ¾ ripe banana, then mix in 3 Tbsp egg whites and 1 Tbsp tahini. Add ¼ cup vanilla protein powder, ¼ cup dry oats, 2 Tbsp raisins, and 2 Tbsp ground flax, and mix well. Scoop batter onto baking sheet and bake for 18 to 22 minutes until golden brown. Makes 2 servings (2-3 cookies per serving). Store remaining in airtight container for Day 8 snack.

DINNER
Delicious Tofu Shakshuka (p. 86)

MEAL PREPPED

SNACK
Yogurt with Pears
Top 1 cup plain Greek yogurt with 1¼ pears, sliced.

Nutrition (per Day): 1,631 calories, 119 g protein, 147g carbohydrate (29 g fiber), 70 g fat

CHAPTER 6 | The Meal Plan

SHOPPING LIST

WEEK 2

Meats & Proteins
8 oz **extra lean beef**
10 oz **boneless, skinless chicken breast**
1 dozen **eggs**
1 pint **egg whites**
1 small container **hummus**
8 oz **lean ground pork**
1 small container **chocolate protein powder**
1 small container **vanilla protein powder**
10 oz **salmon**
8 oz **shrimp**
4 oz **tilapia fillets**
8 oz **extra lean ground turkey**

Dairy
2 quarts **unsweetened almond milk**
1 (32-oz) container **plain Greek yogurt**

Produce
1 package **arugula**
2 bunches **asparagus**
2 **avocados**
15 **bananas**
1 **green bell pepper**
2 **red bell peppers**
1 (16-oz) bag **frozen berries**
½ pint **blueberries**
1 head **Boston lettuce**
1 **carrot**
1 **cauliflower**
1 package **frozen cauliflower**
1 bunch **celery**
1 **cucumber**
1 **fig**
1 head **garlic**
4 **lemons**
1 **lime**
1 **red onion**
1 bunch **parsley**
1 **pear**
1 **pineapple**
1 small package **baby spinach**
1 quart **strawberries**
2 medium **sweet potatoes**
1 **tomato**
1 pint **cherry tomatoes**

Pantry
1 small package **almond flour**
1 (15-oz) can **black beans**
1 small container **cajun seasoning**
1 small package **cashews**
1 small package **chia seeds**
1 small bottle **coconut aminos**
1 small container **coconut butter**
1 small jar **coconut oil**
1 small container **Greek seasoning**
1 small package **ground flax seed**
1 small container **oats**
1 small container **quick-cooking oats**
1 small container **pitted kalamata olives**
1 small jar **all-natural peanut butter**
1 box **quinoa penne pasta**
1 (15-oz) can **pumpkin puree**
1 small container **raisins**
1 small container **sesame seeds**
1 small container **tahini**
1 small package **tapioca flour**
1 (15-oz) can **fire-roasted diced tomatoes**
1 package **brown rice tortillas**
1 small package **chopped walnuts**

BEFORE YOUR GROCERY RUN
Check for leftover ingredients from Week 1 before purchasing new ingredients from the shopping list.

THE LOSE YOUR GUT GUIDE

WEEK 2 MEAL PREP

ON DAY 7

For Yogurt & Berries: Fill 2 airtight containers with 1 cup plain Greek yogurt and 1 cup frozen berries each.

For Yogurt with Pears: Fill 2 airtight containers with 1 cup plain Greek yogurt and ½ pear, sliced, each.

For PB&J Overnight Oats: Follow recipe on page 95.

DAY 8

BREAKFAST
PB&J Overnight Oats (p. 95)
Refrigerate remaining in an airtight container for Day 10 breakfast.

LUNCH
Greek Chicken Salad (p. 101)
Refrigerate remaining in an airtight container for Day 9 dinner.

SNACK
Lemon Tart Smoothie (p. 108)
Refrigerate remaining in an airtight container for Day 10 snack.

DINNER
Blackened Fish Taco Bowls (p. 111)
Refrigerate remaining in an airtight container for Day 9 lunch.

SNACK
LEFTOVERS
Cinnamon Raisin Protein Cookies

Nutrition (per Day): 2,068 calories, 119 g protein, 198 g carbohydrates (47 g fiber), 101 g fat

DAY 9

LEFTOVERS
BREAKFAST
Chocolate Protein Pancakes

LEFTOVERS
LUNCH
Blackened Fish Taco Bowls

MEAL PREPPED
SNACK
Yogurt & Berries
Top 1 cup plain Greek yogurt with 1 cup frozen berries (thawed).

LEFTOVERS
DINNER
Greek Chicken Salad

070

CHAPTER 6 | The Meal Plan

DAY 10

LEFTOVERS

BREAKFAST
PB&J Overnight Oats

LEFTOVERS

SNACK
Lemon Tart Smoothie

LUNCH
Asian Pork Lettuce Wraps
Refrigerate remaining in an airtight container for Day 12 lunch.

DINNER
Ground Beef, Asparagus, and Mashed Sweet Potatoes (p. 104)
Refrigerate remaining in an airtight container for Day 11 lunch.

MEAL PREPPED

SNACK
Yogurt & Berries
Top 1 cup plain Greek yogurt with 1 cup frozen berries (thawed).

Nutrition (Per Day): 1,956 calories, 115 g protein, 183 g carbohydrates (38 g fiber), 94 g fat

SNACK
Banana Cinnamon Smoothie
To a blender, add ½ cup vanilla protein powder, 2 Tbsp ground flax seed, 2 Tbsp chia seeds, 2 frozen bananas, 4 ice cubes, 2 cups water, and ½ tsp cinnamon. Blend until smooth. Makes 1 serving.

Nutrition (per Day): 1,711 calories, 138 g protein, 146 g carbohydrate (34 g fiber), 70g fat

THE LOSE YOUR GUT GUIDE

DAY 11

LEFTOVERS

BREAKFAST
Chocolate Protein Pancakes

LEFTOVERS

LUNCH
Ground Beef, Asparagus, and Mashed Sweet Potatoes

DINNER
Cajun Shrimp Penne (p. 105)
Refrigerate remaining in an airtight container for Day 13 dinner.

MEAL PREPPED

SNACK
Yogurt with Pears
Top 1 cup plain Greek yogurt with ½ pear, sliced.

Nutrition (per Day): 1,658 calories, 17 g protein, 164 g carbohydrate (18 g fiber), 63 g fat

DAY 12

LEFTOVERS

BREAKFAST
PB&J Overnight Oats

MEAL PREPPED

SNACK
Yogurt with Pears
Top 1 cup plain Greek yogurt with ½ pear, sliced.

LEFTOVERS

LUNCH
Asian Pork Lettuce Wraps

SNACK
Berry & Greek Yogurt Smoothie
To a blender, add 1 cup plain Greek yogurt, 2 Tbsp honey, 2 frozen bananas, 1 cup frozen berries, 2 Tbsp ground flax seed, and 2 cups water. Blend until smooth. Makes 2 servings. Refrigerate leftovers in an airtight container for Day 13 lunch.

DINNER
Arugula Salad with Salmon

Heat a skillet over medium heat. Season 6 oz salmon with salt, add to pan skin-side down, and cook for 4 to 5 minutes. Flip and cook for an additional 1 to 2 minutes, until the flesh is opaque throughout. In a small bowl, mix 1 Tbsp extra virgin olive oil and 1 Tbsp lemon juice. Add 2 cups arugula to a plate and top with ½ cucumber, sliced, ½ avocado, sliced, and 1 fig, sliced. Drizzle with dressing and top with salmon.

Nutrition (per Day): 1,930 calories, 121 g protein, 158 g carbohydrates (32 g fiber), 98 g fat

DAY 13

BREAKFAST
Taco Breakfast Bowl (p. 97)

LUNCH
Berry & Greek Yogurt Smoothie (Leftovers) and Hummus & Veggie Snack Box
Eat ½ red bell pepper, sliced, 2 stalks celery, cut

072

CHAPTER 6 | The Meal Plan

into small stalks, ⅓ cup blueberries, and ¼ cup hummus.

LEFTOVERS

DINNER
Cajun Shrimp Penne

SNACK
Pumpkin Pie Protein Smoothie
To a blender, add 2 cups almond milk, 1 cup canned pumpkin puree, 2 frozen bananas, pinch of pumpkin spice, and ½ cup vanilla protein powder. Blend until smooth. Makes 2 servings. Refrigerate remaining in an airtight container for Day 14 snack.

Nutrition (per Day): 1,944 calories, 121 g protein, 235 g carbohydrates (36 g fiber), 67 g fat

DAY 14

BREAKFAST
Banana Nut Pancakes (p. 98)
Refrigerate remaining in an airtight container for Day 15 breakfast.

SNACK
Pumpkin Pie Protein Smoothie (Leftovers) and Cinnamon Raisin Protein Cookies
Preheat the oven to 350°F and line a baking sheet with parchment paper. In a medium bowl, mash ¾ ripe banana, then mix in 3 Tbsp egg whites and 1 Tbsp tahini. Add ¼ cup vanilla protein powder, ¼ cup dry oats, 2 Tbsp raisins, and 2 Tbsp ground flax, and mix well. Scoop batter onto baking sheet and bake for 18 to 22 minutes until golden brown. Makes 2 servings (2-3 cookies per serving). Store remaining in airtight container for Day 20 snack.

LUNCH
Breakfast Taco Nachos (p. 107)

DINNER
One-Pan Hawaiian Salmon (p. 117)

Nutrition (per Day): 2,200 calories, 135 g protein, 218 g carbohydrates (41 g fiber), 102 g fat

THE LOSE YOUR GUT GUIDE

WEEK 3 SHOPPING LIST

WEEK 3

Meats & Proteins

11 oz **stewing beef**

5 oz **chicken**

2 oz **baked chicken breast**

1 (15-oz) **chicken breast**

1 dozen **eggs**

1 container **hummus**

24 oz **ground lamb**

1 small package **chocolate protein powder**

1 small package **vanilla protein powder**

8 oz **shrimp**

1 can **tuna**

1 can **flaked tuna**

Dairy

1 quart **unsweetened almond milk**

2 (32-oz) containers **plain Greek yogurt**

Produce

1 **avocado**

5 **bananas**

1 **bell pepper**

1 **red bell pepper**

1 **yellow bell pepper**

2 (16-oz) bags **frozen berries**

1 (16-oz) bag **frozen blueberries**

2 heads **broccoli**

4½ cups **Brussels sprouts**

1 package **baby carrots**

1 **cauliflower**

1 pint **cherry tomatoes**

1 package **coleslaw mix**

1 **cucumber**

1 head **garlic**

1 can or 1 frozen package **green peas**

1 bunch **kale**

1 **lemon**

1 **lime**

1 package **mushrooms**

1 **sweet onion**

1 bunch **parsley**

1 **pear**

1 large **pomegranate**

1 bunch **radishes**

2¼ cups **snap peas**

1 package **spinach**

1 package **baby spinach**

1 bunch **thyme**

2 **zucchini**

Pantry

1 small jar **almond butter**

1 package **almond flour**

1 package **raw almonds**

1 small container **whole-grain bread crumbs**

1 quart **beef broth**

1 small package **brown rice flour**

1 package **cacao nibs**

1 package **chia seeds**

1 (15.5-oz) can **chickpeas**

1 package **chickpea flour**

1 package **organic dark chocolate chips**

1 package **coconut flour**

1 (13.5-oz) can **coconut milk**

1 small jar **coconut oil**

1 small package **ground flax seed**

1 bag **lentils**

1 package **whole-wheat pita**

1 package **raw pumpkin seeds**

1 package **quinoa**

1 small container **sesame seeds**

1 jar **sunflower seed butter**

1 package **tapioca flour**

1 small package **chopped walnuts**

BEFORE YOUR GROCERY RUN

Check for leftover ingredients from Week 2 before purchasing new ingredients from the shopping list.

CHAPTER 6 | The Meal Plan

WEEK 3 MEAL PREP

ON DAY 14

For Yogurt & Berries: Fill 2 airtight containers with 1 cup plain Greek yogurt and 1 cup frozen berries each.

DAY 15

LEFTOVERS
BREAKFAST
Banana Nut Pancakes

LUNCH
Spring Salad
In a large bowl, combine ½ cup lentils, ¾ cup snap peas, ¼ cup green peas, ½ cup spinach, and ½ can flaked tuna. Then, in a small jar, combine 1 Tbsp each vinegar, olive oil, mustard, pinch of salt, and pepper. Put lid on and shake well. Pour dressing over salad and toss well. Makes 1 serving.

MEAL PREPPED
SNACK
Yogurt & Berries
Top 1 cup plain Greek yogurt with 1 cup frozen berries (thawed).

DINNER
One-Pan Lamb Meatballs & Veggies (p. 119)
Refrigerate remaining in an airtight container for Day 16 lunch.

SNACK
Blueberry Protein Smoothie
To a blender, add ½ cup vanilla protein powder, 2 Tbsp ground flax seed, 2 cups frozen blueberries, 2 cups baby spinach, and 2 cups water. Blend until smooth. Makes 2 servings. Refrigerate remaining in an airtight container for Day 16 snack.

Nutrition (per Day): 1,769 calories, 117 g protein, 148 g carbohydrates (37 g fiber), 87 g fat

DAY 16

BREAKFAST
Paleo Overnight Oats (p. 113)
Refrigerate remaining in an airtight container for Day 18 breakfast.

LEFTOVERS
LUNCH
One-Pan Lamb Meatballs & Veggies

LEFTOVERS
SNACK
Blueberry Protein Smoothie

DINNER
One-Pan Chicken Stir-Fry (p. 120)
Refrigerate remaining in an airtight container for Day 17 lunch.

Nutrition (per Day): 1,951 calories, 108 g protein, 99 g carbohydrates (34 g fiber), 92 g fat

075

DAY 17

BREAKFAST
Banana Nut Pancakes (p. 98)
Refrigerate remaining in an airtight container for Day 19 breakfast.

LEFTOVERS

LUNCH
One-Pan Chicken Stir-Fry

DINNER
Slow-Cooker Beef Stew (p. 123)
Refrigerate remaining in an airtight container for Day 20 dinner.

SNACK
Yogurt & Berries
Top 1 cup plain Greek yogurt with 1 cup frozen berries (thawed).

Nutrition (per Day): 1,636 calories, 120 g protein, 139 g carbohydrates (24 g fiber), 73 g fat

DAY 18

LEFTOVERS

BREAKFAST
Paleo Overnight Oats

LUNCH
One-Pan Lamb Meatballs & Veggies (p. 119)

DINNER
Popcorn Chicken & Coconut Zucchini Fries (p. 110)

SNACK
Yogurt with Pear
Top 1 cup plain Greek yogurt with ½ pear, sliced.

Nutrition (per Day): 1,597 calories, 109 g protein, 85 g carbohydrates (27 g fiber), 96 g fat

CHAPTER 6 | The Meal Plan

DAY 19

LEFTOVERS

BREAKFAST
Banana Nut Pancakes

LUNCH
Kale Caesar Salad
Preheat the oven to 400°F. Chop off top of ¼ head of garlic, drizzle with 1 Tbsp olive oil, and wrap in foil. Bake for 30 minutes. When garlic is cool, squeeze flesh out of skin. To a blender, add garlic, 1 Tbsp each olive oil, lemon juice, mustard, and pinch of salt. Blend until creamy. To a large bowl, add 1 cup kale leaves, 2 Tbsp radishes, ½ cup cherry tomatoes, and 1 Tbsp pumpkin seeds. Drizzle with dressing and toss well. Top with 2 oz baked chicken breast and fresh ground pepper.

DINNER
Grilled Shrimp Salad (p. 124)

LEFTOVERS

SNACK
Edible Chocolate Chip Cookie Dough
In a food processor, place 1 cup chickpeas, ¼ cup sunflower seed butter, 2 Tbsp maple syrup, and ½ tsp vanilla extract. Process until smooth. Then, transfer cookie dough to a bowl and stir in ¼ cup dark chocolate chips. Roll into an even number of balls. Makes 2 servings. Refrigerate remaining in an airtight container for Day 20 snack.

Nutrition (per Day): 1,944 calories, 103 g protein, 129 g carbohydrates (26 g fiber), 119 g fat

DAY 20

BREAKFAST
Brownie Protein Pancakes (p. 114)

LUNCH
Berry & Greek Yogurt Smoothie and Cinnamon Raisin Protein Cookies (Leftovers)
Berry & Greek Yogurt Smoothie: To a blender, add ½ cup plain Greek yogurt, 1 Tbsp honey, 1 frozen banana, ½ cup frozen berries, 1 Tbsp ground flax seed, and 1 cup water. Blend until smooth.

LEFTOVERS

DINNER
Slow-Cooker Beef Stew

LEFTOVERS

SNACK
Edible Chocolate Chip Cookie Dough

Nutrition (per Day): 1,935 calories, 111 g protein, 212 g carbohydrates (33 g fiber), 74 g fat

077

THE LOSE YOUR GUT GUIDE

DAY 21

BREAKFAST
Paleo Overnight Oats (p. 113)

LUNCH
Tuna Salad Plate
In a small bowl, mix 1 can tuna, ½ avocado, ¼ cup plain Greek yogurt, ¼ cucumber, chopped, and pinch of salt. Season with pepper.

`MEAL PREPPED`

SNACK
Yogurt & Berries
Top 1 cup plain Greek yogurt with 1 cup frozen berries (thawed).

DINNER
Veggie Pita Pizza with Hummus
Preheat the oven to 350°F and line a baking sheet with parchment paper. In a large skillet, heat 1 Tbsp olive oil over medium-high heat. Cook ½ bell pepper and ½ zucchini, sliced, until tender and lightly browned. Spread ½ cup hummus over a whole-wheat pita and top with bell pepper and zucchini. Place onto baking sheet and bake for 8 to 10 minutes or until pita is toasted.

SNACK
Banana Cinnamon Smoothie
To a blender, add ½ cup vanilla protein powder, 2 Tbsp ground flax seed, 2 Tbsp chia seeds, 2 frozen bananas, 4 ice cubes, 2 cups water, ½ tsp cinnamon. Blend until smooth. Makes 1 serving.

Nutrition (per Day): 1,840 calories, 115 g protein, 56 g carbohydrates (46 g fiber), 95 g fat

CHAPTER 6 | The Meal Plan

Spicy Quinoa Tacos.....**80**
Overnight Blueberry Oat Success.....**82**
Protein Breakfast Power Bowl.....**85**
Delicious Tofu Shakshuka.....**86**
Chocolate Protein Pancakes.....**88**
Anti-Inflammatory Chicken Salad.....**91**
Shrimp Zoodle Stir-Fry.....**92**
PB&J Overnight Oats.....**95**
Taco Breakfast Bowl.....**97**
Banana Nut Pancakes.....**98**
Greek Chicken Salad.....**101**
Asian Pork Lettuce Wraps.....**102**
Ground Beef, Asparagus, and Mashed Sweet Potatoes.....**104**
Cajun Shrimp Penne.....**105**
Breakfast Taco Nachos.....**107**
Lemon Tart Smoothie.....**108**
Popcorn Chicken & Coconut Zucchini Fries.....**110**
Blackened Fish Taco Bowls.....**111**
Paleo Overnight Oats.....**113**
Brownie Protein Pancakes.....**114**
One-Pan Hawaiian Salmon.....**117**
One-Pan Lamb Meatballs & Veggies.....**119**
One-Pan Chicken Stir-Fry.....**120**
Slow-Cooker Beef Stew.....**123**
Grilled Shrimp Salad.....**124**

079

THE LOSE YOUR GUT GUIDE

SPICY QUINOA TACOS

PREP TIME: 10 MIN   COOK TIME: 35 MIN

WHAT YOU'LL NEED

¼ CUP WATER

1 CUP COOKED, DRAINED, AND RINSED BLACK BEANS

¾ CUP DICED TOMATOES (FRESH OR CANNED)

½ CUP CORN (FRESH, CANNED, OR FROZEN)

½ TSP CUMIN

¼ TSP PAPRIKA

¾ TSP CHILI POWDER

¼ TSP SEA SALT

⅓ CUP UNCOOKED QUINOA

2 CORN TORTILLAS

1 CUP BABY SPINACH

½ AVOCADO, DICED

1 TBSP PLAIN GREEK YOGURT

HOW TO MAKE IT

1. In a large pot, add water, black beans, tomatoes, corn, cumin, paprika, chili powder, and salt. Bring to a simmer.

2. Add quinoa and cook for 12 to 15 minutes more.

3. Place each corn tortilla wrap on a plate and top with spinach, avocado, Greek yogurt, and quinoa filling.

MAKES 2 SERVINGS

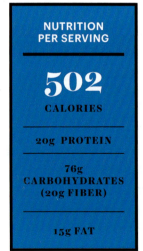

NUTRITION PER SERVING

502 CALORIES

20g PROTEIN

76g CARBOHYDRATES (20g FIBER)

15g FAT

080

THE LOSE YOUR GUT GUIDE

OVERNIGHT BLUEBERRY OAT SUCCESS

PREP TIME: 25 MIN   COOK TIME: 8 HR OR OVERNIGHT

WHAT YOU'LL NEED

1½ CUPS OATS

1½ CUPS UNSWEETENED ALMOND MILK

2 TBSP CHIA SEEDS

2 TBSP MAPLE SYRUP

1 TSP CINNAMON

½ CUP WATER

1 CUP BLUEBERRIES

1 CUP SLIVERED ALMONDS

HOW TO MAKE IT

1. Combine the oats, almond milk, chia seeds, maple syrup, cinnamon, and water in a large plastic container. Stir well to mix. Seal and place in the fridge overnight (or for at least 8 hours).

2. Remove oats from the fridge. Use 3 single-serving-size mason jars, and place a large spoonful of the oat mix in the bottom of each, then a layer of blueberries followed by a layer of slivered almonds. Repeat until all ingredients are used. Enjoy hot or cold!

MAKES 3 SERVINGS

NUTRITION PER SERVING

414 CALORIES

14g PROTEIN

43g CARBOHYDRATES (10g FIBER)

23g FAT

CHAPTER 6 | The Meal Plan

PROTEIN BREAKFAST POWER BOWL

PREP TIME: 25 MIN   COOK TIME: 5 MIN

WHAT YOU'LL NEED

¼ CUP UNCOOKED QUINOA

¾ CUP WATER

2 EGGS

2 CUPS BABY SPINACH

⅓ CUP HALVED CHERRY TOMATOES

½ AVOCADO, MASHED

⅛ TSP SEA SALT (OR MORE TO TASTE)

HOW TO MAKE IT

1. In a medium-size saucepan, add quinoa and water and bring to a low boil. Once boiling, reduce heat to a simmer, cover, and let cook for about 12 to 15 minutes. When done, remove the pot from the heat and fluff the quinoa with a fork.

2. In a medium skillet over medium-low, make scrambled eggs. Remove and place on a plate.

3. Add the spinach to the same pan and heat over low until wilted. Remove from heat.

4. Add quinoa to a bowl and add the eggs, spinach, cherry tomatoes, and mashed avocado.

5. Season to taste with salt.

NUTRITION PER SERVING

483 CALORIES

23g PROTEIN

41g CARBOHYDRATES (12g FIBER)

27g FAT

MAKES 2 SERVINGS

THE LOSE YOUR GUT GUIDE

DELICIOUS TOFU SHAKSHUKA

PREP TIME: 10 MIN   COOK TIME: 20 MIN

WHAT YOU'LL NEED

3½ OZ FIRM TOFU, PAT DRY

1 TBSP WATER

¼ RED BELL PEPPER, CHOPPED

½ TSP PAPRIKA

¼ TSP CUMIN

⅔ CUP FIRE-ROASTED DICED TO-MATOES, WITH JUICES

3 TBSP FINELY CHOPPED PARSLEY, DIVIDED

SEA SALT & BLACK PEPPER, TO TASTE

¼ AVOCADO, SLICED

HOW TO MAKE IT

1. Preheat the oven to 375°F. Slice ¾ of the tofu into even pieces. Crumble the remaining ¼ of the tofu. Keep separate and set aside.

2. In an oven-safe skillet over medium, heat the water. Sauté the red bell pepper until slightly tender, about 3 to 4 minutes.

3. Stir in the paprika and cumin and cook for 1 minute. Stir in the diced tomatoes, ¾ of the parsley, salt, and pepper. Place the tofu slices on top and cover with a lid. Simmer for 10 minutes.

4. Remove the lid and transfer the skillet to the oven. Bake for 10 minutes uncovered or until the tofu has crisped on top.

5. Garnish with the crumbled tofu, remaining parsley, and avocado. Divide into bowls and enjoy!

NUTRITION PER SERVING

217
CALORIES

13g PROTEIN

16g CARBOHYDRATES (7g FIBER)

13g FAT

MAKES 2 SERVINGS

THE LOSE YOUR GUT GUIDE

CHOCOLATE PROTEIN PANCAKES

PREP TIME: 10 MIN   COOK TIME: 20 MIN

WHAT YOU'LL NEED

3 RIPE BANANAS

6 EGGS

¾ CUP CHOCOLATE PROTEIN POWDER

1½ TBSP COCONUT OIL

HOW TO MAKE IT

1. In a large bowl, mash the bananas. Then add the eggs and protein powder. Mix well until a batter forms.

2. In a large skillet over medium, melt the coconut oil. Once hot, pour pancake batter into the skillet, about ¼ cup at a time. Cook each side about 2 to 3 minutes or until browned.

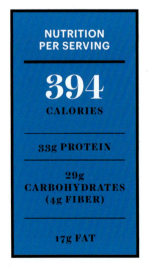

NUTRITION PER SERVING

394 CALORIES

33g PROTEIN

29g CARBOHYDRATES (4g FIBER)

17g FAT

MAKES 3 SERVINGS

CHAPTER 6 | The Meal Plan

ANTI-INFLAMMATORY CHICKEN SALAD

PREP TIME: 10 MIN   COOK TIME: 30 MIN

WHAT YOU'LL NEED

1 LB SKINLESS, BONELESS CHICKEN BREAST

1 TBSP AVOCADO OIL

1 TSP TURMERIC

SEA SALT & BLACK PEPPER

2 CUPS BABY SPINACH

1 CUP CHERRY TOMATOES

½ CUCUMBER, SLICED

HOW TO MAKE IT

1. Preheat the oven to 400°F and line a baking sheet with parchment paper.
2. Toss the chicken breast in the avocado oil, turmeric, salt, and pepper. Transfer to the baking sheet and cook for 25 to 30 minutes or until the chicken is cooked through.
3. Divide the spinach, cherry tomatoes, and cucumber between plates. Top with the chicken and enjoy!

NUTRITION PER SERVING

369 CALORIES

53g PROTEIN

8g CARBOHYDRATES (2g FIBER)

13g FAT

MAKES 2 SERVINGS

THE LOSE YOUR GUT GUIDE

SHRIMP ZOODLE STIR-FRY

PREP TIME: 10 MIN   COOK TIME: 30 MIN

WHAT YOU'LL NEED

- ⅓ CUP ORGANIC VEGETABLE OR CHICKEN BROTH
- 1⅓ TBSP TAMARI
- 2 LARGE ZUCCHINI
- 1⅓ TBSP COCONUT OIL, DIVIDED
- 2 MINCED GARLIC CLOVES
- 1 TSP GRATED GINGER
- 10⅔ OZ SHRIMP, PEELED AND DEVEINED
- ⅔ LARGE YELLOW BELL PEPPER, SLICED
- ⅔ CUP MATCHSTICK CARROTS
- 2⅔ TBSP DICED RED ONION
- 2 CUPS ASPARAGUS (WOODY ENDS SNAPPED OFF)
- 2 TSP SESAME SEEDS

HOW TO MAKE IT

1. In a small bowl, combine the broth and tamari. Set aside.
2. Spiralize your zucchini into noodles and set aside.
3. In a large frying pan over medium-low, place half of the coconut oil. Add the garlic and ginger and sauté for a minute. Add the shrimp and sauté for about 3 minutes or until cooked through. (Note: Shrimp should be pink on all sides.) Transfer the shrimp to a bowl and set aside.
4. Increase heat to medium. Add remaining coconut oil to the pan along with the bell peppers, carrots, red onion, and asparagus. Sauté for 4 minutes or until veggies are slightly tender. Add your broth/tamari mix and stir for another 4 minutes.
5. Return the shrimp to the pan along with the zucchini noodles. Use tongs to toss and coat for 1 to 2 minutes or until zucchini noodles are slightly softened.
6. Divide stir-fry onto plates and sprinkle with sesame seeds.

MAKES 2 SERVINGS

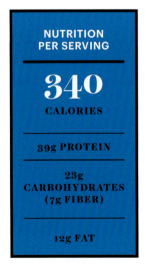

NUTRITION PER SERVING

340 CALORIES

39g PROTEIN

23g CARBOHYDRATES (7g FIBER)

12g FAT

CHAPTER 6 | The Meal Plan

PB&J OVERNIGHT OATS

PREP TIME: 10 MIN COOK TIME: 8 HR

WHAT YOU'LL NEED

½ CUP ALL-NATURAL PEANUT BUTTER, DIVIDED

¼ CUP MAPLE SYRUP, DIVIDED

2 CUPS UNSWEETENED ALMOND MILK

1½ CUPS QUICK-COOKING OATS

1½ TBSP CHIA SEEDS

3 CUPS FINELY CHOPPED STRAWBERRIES

HOW TO MAKE IT

1. In a medium bowl, add half of the peanut butter and half of the maple syrup. Slowly whisk in almond milk until combined.

2. Stir in the oats and chia seeds until combined. Cover and let sit for at least 3 hours or overnight.

3. In a separate bowl, add chopped strawberries and remaining maple syrup. Stir to coat the strawberries in the syrup, then cover and let rest in the fridge until oats are ready.

4. To serve, divide the peanut butter oats evenly between 3 mason jars. Top with equal amounts of the sweetened strawberries (and their juices) and remaining peanut butter.

MAKES 3 SERVINGS

NUTRITION PER SERVING

567
CALORIES

17g PROTEIN

71g CARBOHYDRATES (11g FIBER)

27g FAT

CHAPTER 6 | The Meal Plan

TACO BREAKFAST BOWL

PREP TIME: 10 MIN   COOK TIME: 25 MIN

WHAT YOU'LL NEED

⅓ TSP EXTRA VIRGIN OLIVE OIL

4 OZ EXTRA LEAN GROUND TURKEY

1½ TSP CHILI POWDER

¼ TSP OREGANO

¼ TSP CUMIN

¼ TSP BLACK PEPPER

¼ TSP SEA SALT

2 TBSP WATER

1 FRIED EGG

1 CUP CHOPPED BABY SPINACH

¼ GREEN BELL PEPPER, DICED

¼ TOMATO, DICED

¼ AVOCADO, MASHED

HOW TO MAKE IT

1. In a medium skillet over medium, heat olive oil. Add the ground turkey and sauté until cooked through. Break up the meat as it is cooking. Once it is cooked through, add the chili powder, oregano, cumin, black pepper, and sea salt. Add the water and sauté for another minute, mixing well. Reduce heat to the lowest setting and let simmer while you prepare the rest or until all water has been absorbed.
2. Fry the egg and set aside.
3. Divide the spinach between bowls. Top with diced green pepper, tomato, mashed avocado, taco meat, and fried egg.

NUTRITION PER SERVING

370
CALORIES

31g PROTEIN

11g
CARBOHYDRATES
(7g FIBER)

24g FAT

MAKES 2 SERVINGS

THE LOSE YOUR GUT GUIDE

BANANA NUT PANCAKES

PREP TIME: 15 MIN   COOK TIME: 15 MIN

WHAT YOU'LL NEED

2 BANANAS
½ CUP UNSWEETENED ALMOND MILK
2 CUPS ALMOND FLOUR
3 EGGS
1 TBSP BAKING POWDER
1 TBSP TAPIOCA FLOUR
1 TBSP COCONUT OIL
½ CUP CHOPPED WALNUTS
⅓ CUP MAPLE SYRUP

HOW TO MAKE IT

1. In a medium bowl, mash 1 banana with a fork. Add almond milk, almond flour, eggs, baking powder, and tapioca flour. Mix until thoroughly combined.

2. In a medium skillet over low-medium, heat coconut oil. Once hot, pour pancakes in the skillet, about 3 to 4 inches wide. Cook for about 3 to 4 minutes per side (or until middle begins to bubble).

3. Transfer to plates and top with the remaining banana (sliced), walnuts, and maple syrup.

MAKES 2 SERVINGS

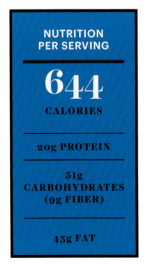

NUTRITION PER SERVING

644 CALORIES

20g PROTEIN

51g CARBOHYDRATES (9g FIBER)

45g FAT

CHAPTER 6 | The Meal Plan

GREEK CHICKEN SALAD

PREP TIME: 15 MIN   COOK TIME: 30 MIN

WHAT YOU'LL NEED

1 TBSP GREEK SEASONING

JUICE OF ½ LEMON

2 TBSP EXTRA VIRGIN OLIVE OIL, DIVIDED

10 OZ BONELESS, SKINLESS CHICKEN BREAST

1½ CUPS HALVED CHERRY TOMATOES

½ CUCUMBER, DICED

2 TBSP FINELY DICED RED ONION

½ CUP CHOPPED PITTED KALAMATA OLIVES

1½ TBSP BALSAMIC VINEGAR

SEA SALT & BLACK PEPPER, TO TASTE

HOW TO MAKE IT

1. In a shallow bowl or resealable food storage bag, combine the Greek seasoning, lemon juice, and ¼ of the olive oil. Add the chicken breasts and marinate for 20 minutes or overnight.

2. Preheat a grill or skillet over medium. Remove chicken from the marinade and cook for 10 to 15 minutes per side, or until chicken is cooked through.

3. While the chicken is cooking, make the salad: Combine the cherry tomatoes, cucumbers, red onion, olives, balsamic vinegar, remaining olive oil, salt, and pepper. Mix well.

4. Divide the salad and chicken between plates.

MAKES 2 SERVINGS

NUTRITION PER SERVING

376
CALORIES

34g PROTEIN

13g CARBOHYDRATES (2g FIBER)

21g FAT

THE LOSE YOUR GUT GUIDE

ASIAN PORK LETTUCE WRAPS

PREP TIME: 15 MIN   COOK TIME: 30 MIN

NUTRITION PER SERVING

299

CALORIES

21g PROTEIN

7g CARBOHYDRATES (1g FIBER)

21g FAT

WHAT YOU'LL NEED

½ TSP AVOCADO OIL

1 MINCED GARLIC CLOVE

8 OZ LEAN GROUND PORK

1 TBSP COCONUT AMINOS

½ TSP SESAME OIL

½ TSP HONEY

½ HEAD BOSTON LETTUCE (LEAVES SEPARATED)

1 CARROT, SHREDDED

½ TSP SESAME SEEDS (OPTIONAL, FOR GARNISH)

HOW TO MAKE IT

1. In a skillet over medium, heat the avocado oil. Once the pan is hot, add the garlic and cook for 1 minute. Add the pork and stir to combine. Cook for 6 to 8 minutes, until cooked through. Drain any excess fat and return to the stove.
2. In a small bowl, mix together the coconut aminos, sesame oil, and honey. Add the sauce to the pork and stir to combine, cooking for another 1 to 2 minutes.
3. Put the pork mixture into individual lettuce leaves. Top with shredded carrot and sesame seeds, if using.

MAKES 2 SERVINGS

THE LOSE YOUR GUT GUIDE

GROUND BEEF, ASPARAGUS & MASHED SWEET POTATOES

PREP TIME: 15 MIN   COOK TIME: 10 MIN

WHAT YOU'LL NEED

2 MEDIUM SWEET POTATOES, PEELED AND CHOPPED

2 CUPS ASPARAGUS

SALT

½ CUP OIL

8 OZ EXTRA LEAN BEEF

HOW TO MAKE IT

1. In a steamer basket over boiling water, set the sweet potatoes. Cover and steam for 15 minutes, or until tender. Transfer sweet potatoes to a bowl.
2. Steam 2 cups asparagus for about 3 to 5 minutes for thin asparagus or 6 to 8 minutes for thick asparagus and set aside.
3. Add a pinch of salt to sweet potatoes and mash until creamy.
4. In a large pan over medium, heat the oil. Cook the beef, breaking it up as it cooks. Season with a pinch of salt and drain any excess liquid.
5. Divide the mashed sweet potato, asparagus, and beef onto plates or into containers.

MAKES 2 SERVINGS

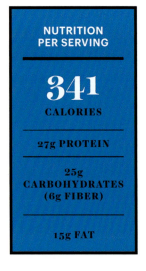

NUTRITION PER SERVING

341 CALORIES

27g PROTEIN

25g CARBOHYDRATES (6g FIBER)

15g FAT

CHAPTER 6 | The Meal Plan

CAJUN SHRIMP PENNE

PREP TIME: 5 MIN   COOK TIME: 15 MIN

WHAT YOU'LL NEED

- 2 CUPS QUINOA PENNE PASTA
- ⅓ CUP CASHEWS
- ⅓ CUP WATER
- 8 OZ SHRIMP
- 1½ TBSP CAJUN SEASONING, DIVIDED
- 2 TBSP EXTRA VIRGIN OLIVE OIL, DIVIDED
- 3 SPEARS OR ¾ CUP CHOPPED ASPARAGUS
- ¼ TSP SEA SALT
- 1 MINCED GARLIC CLOVE
- 1 CUP FIRE-ROASTED DICED TOMATOES
- SALT AND BLACK PEPPER
- PARSLEY, FOR SERVING

HOW TO MAKE IT

1. In a medium pot, bring water to a boil and cook quinoa penne pasta according to package directions. Set aside.

2. To a blender, add cashews and water. Blend on high for about 1 to 2 minutes until very smooth. Set aside.

3. In a medium bowl, toss shrimp with ½ the cajun seasoning and 1½ tsp olive oil. Set aside.

4. In a cast-iron skillet over medium, add 1½ tsp olive oil along with the asparagus and sea salt. Cook, flipping the asparagus often, about 4 minutes total. Remove from the pan and set aside. Add shrimp to the pan and cook over medium for 3 to 4 minutes, flipping halfway through, until cooked. Remove and set aside.

5. Add remaining 1 Tbsp of the oil to the pan and add the cooked pasta. Over medium-low heat, cook the garlic for 30 seconds. Then, add the tomatoes and remaining cajun seasoning, stir to combine. Allow it to just warm, about 1 to 2 minutes, then add the cashew cream, pasta, and asparagus to the pot. Toss to combine.

6. Divide onto plates, top with shrimp, parsley, and season with salt and pepper.

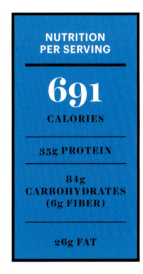

NUTRITION PER SERVING

691 CALORIES

35g PROTEIN

84g CARBOHYDRATES (6g FIBER)

26g FAT

MAKES 2 SERVINGS

CHAPTER 6 | The Meal Plan

BREAKFAST TACO NACHOS

PREP TIME: 15 MIN   COOK TIME: 30 MIN

WHAT YOU'LL NEED

1½ BROWN RICE TORTILLAS

⅓ TSP EXTRA VIRGIN OLIVE OIL

4 OZ EXTRA LEAN GROUND TURKEY

¾ TSP CHILI POWDER

¼ TSP OREGANO

¼ TSP CUMIN

¼ TSP BLACK PEPPER

¼ TSP SEA SALT

2 TBSP WATER

1 EGG

1 TBSP OLIVE OIL

¼ GREEN BELL PEPPER, DICED

¼ TOMATO, DICED

¼ AVOCADO, DICED

HOW TO MAKE IT

1. Preheat the oven to 415°F. Slice tortillas into 8 pieces using a pizza cutter. Place on a baking sheet and bake for 6 minutes. Remove from the oven and set aside.

2. Meanwhile, heat a skillet over medium. Add the olive oil and ground turkey and sauté to cook through, breaking the meat up as it cooks. Once cooked through, add the chili powder, oregano, cumin, black pepper, and sea salt. Add the water and sauté for another minute as you mix well. Reduce heat to the lowest setting and let simmer while you prepare the rest or until all water has been absorbed.

3. Fry your egg with 1 Tbsp oil and set aside.

4. Place tortilla chips in a bowl and top with diced green pepper, tomato, avocado, turkey, and fried egg.

MAKES 1 SERVING

NUTRITION PER SERVING

582
CALORIES

34g PROTEIN

49g CARBOHYDRATES (10g FIBER)

28g FAT

THE LOSE YOUR GUT GUIDE

LEMON TART SMOOTHIE

PREP TIME: 5 MIN   COOK TIME: 5 MIN

WHAT YOU'LL NEED

JUICE OF 2 LEMONS

2 FROZEN PEELED BANANAS

2 CUPS FROZEN CAULIFLOWER

¼ CUP COCONUT BUTTER

½ CUP VANILLA PROTEIN POWDER

3 CUPS UNSWEETENED ALMOND MILK

HOW TO MAKE IT

Place all ingredients in your blender and blend until smooth.

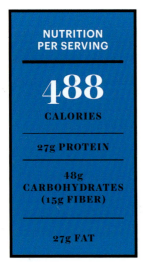

NUTRITION PER SERVING

488 CALORIES

27g PROTEIN

48g CARBOHYDRATES (15g FIBER)

27g FAT

MAKES 2 SERVINGS

THE LOSE YOUR GUT GUIDE

POPCORN CHICKEN & COCONUT ZUCCHINI FRIES

PREP TIME: 10 MIN   COOK TIME: 15 MIN

WHAT YOU'LL NEED

5 OZ CUBED CHICKEN

½ CUP GREEK YOGURT

SALT

½ CUP WHOLE-GRAIN BREAD CRUMBS

2 TBSP COCONUT MILK

2 TBSP COCONUT FLOUR

1 ZUCCHINI

HOW TO MAKE IT

1. Preheat the oven to 450°F and line a baking sheet with parchment paper.
2. Make chicken: In a large bowl, toss chicken with Greek yogurt and pinch of salt. Transfer chicken to a separate bowl of bread crumbs and coat evenly. Place on the baking sheet.
3. Make zucchini fries: Pour coconut milk into a small bowl. In a separate bowl, combine coconut flour and pinch of salt.
4. Slice zucchini into strips. Dip each zucchini strip in coconut milk, then salted coconut flour. Place on the baking sheet.
5. Bake both the chicken and zucchini for 12 to 15 minutes or until chicken is cooked through and zucchini is golden brown, flipping the zucchini halfway.

MAKES 1 SERVING

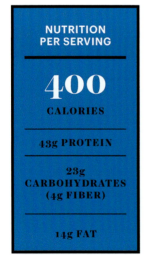

NUTRITION PER SERVING

400 CALORIES

43g PROTEIN

23g CARBOHYDRATES (4g FIBER)

14g FAT

CHAPTER 6 | The Meal Plan

BLACKENED FISH TACO BOWLS

PREP TIME: 5 MIN   COOK TIME: 10 MIN

WHAT YOU'LL NEED

- ½ HEAD CAULIFLOWER, CHOPPED INTO FLORETS
- ¼ AVOCADO
- 4 TBSP OLIVE OIL, DIVIDED
- JUICE OF ½ LEMON
- 2 TBSP WATER
- 1½ TSP CHILI POWDER
- 1½ TSP CUMIN
- ¼ TSP CAYENNE
- ½ TSP PAPRIKA
- ¼ TSP SEA SALT
- ¼ TSP BLACK PEPPER
- 4 OZ TILAPIA FILLETS
- 2 TBSP DICED RED ONION
- ¼ DICED GREEN PEPPER
- 1 CUP BLACK BEANS
- LIME WEDGES, FOR SERVING

HOW TO MAKE IT

1. In a food processor or with a box grater, rice the cauliflower. Set aside in a bowl.

2. In the food processor, combine the avocado, 2 Tbsp olive oil, lemon juice, and water. Blend until smooth and set aside in a jar.

3. In a small bowl, combine chili powder, cumin, cayenne, paprika, sea salt, and black pepper. Sprinkle over both sides of the tilapia fillets.

4. Grease a large cast-iron skillet with 2 Tbsp olive oil and heat on medium high. Add the fillets and sear 3 to 4 minutes per side, or until fish is completely cooked through. (Note: Fish is done when it flakes with a fork.) Remove from heat, chop, and set aside.

5. Divide cauliflower rice in bowls and top with red onion, green pepper, and black beans. Add the tilapia, drizzle with dressing, and serve with lime wedges.

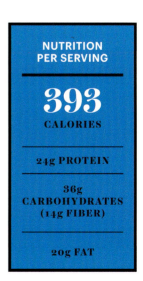

NUTRITION PER SERVING

393 CALORIES

24g PROTEIN

36g CARBOHYDRATES (14g FIBER)

20g FAT

MAKES 2 SERVINGS

CHAPTER 6 | The Meal Plan

PALEO OVERNIGHT OATS

PREP TIME: 5 MIN   COOK TIME: 4 HR

WHAT YOU'LL NEED

1 CUP RAW ALMONDS

½ CUP RAW PUMPKIN SEEDS

1 TBSP GROUND FLAX SEEDS

2 TBSP CHIA SEEDS

1½ CUPS UNSWEETENED ALMOND MILK

¼ TSP GROUND CINNAMON

3 TBSP POMEGRANATE SEEDS

3 TBSP CACAO NIBS

3 TBSP ALMOND BUTTER

HOW TO MAKE IT

1. In a blender, add the almonds, pumpkin seeds, and flax seeds and process until coarsely ground. Transfer to a large glass jar along with the chia seeds, almond milk, and cinnamon. Place in the fridge overnight or for at least 4 hours.

2. In the morning, divide into 3 jars and top with pomegranate seeds, cacao nibs, and almond butter. Enjoy hot or cold! Feel free to throw in microwave for about 2 minutes.

MAKES 3 SERVINGS

NUTRITION PER SERVING

591
CALORIES

21g PROTEIN

26g CARBOHYDRATES (16g FIBER)

49g FAT

THE LOSE YOUR GUT GUIDE

BROWNIE PROTEIN PANCAKES

PREP TIME: 10 MIN COOK TIME: 20 MIN

NUTRITION PER SERVING

444
CALORIES

29g PROTEIN

37 g CARBOHYDRATES (6g FIBER)

19g FAT

WHAT YOU'LL NEED

1 TBSP GROUND FLAX SEED

3 TBSP WATER

¼ CUP CHICKPEA FLOUR

¼ CUP CHOCOLATE PROTEIN POWDER

1½ TSP COCOA POWDER

1½ TSP BAKING POWDER

½ CUP UNSWEETENED ALMOND MILK (OR WATER)

2 TBSP ORGANIC DARK CHOCO-LATE CHIPS

¾ TSP COCONUT OIL

HOW TO MAKE IT

1. In a small bowl, whisk together the ground flax seed and water. Set aside to thicken for about 5 minutes.
2. In a medium bowl, combine the chickpea flour, protein powder, cocoa powder, and baking powder.
3. Add the almond milk and flax mixture to the dry ingredients. Mix well until a smooth batter forms. Fold in the chocolate chips.
4. In a nonstick skillet over medium, heat the coconut oil. Spoon the batter into the pan in ¼-cup portions. Cook pancakes for about 3 to 4 minutes per side.

MAKES 2 SERVINGS

CHAPTER 6 | The Meal Plan

ONE-PAN HAWAIIAN SALMON

PREP TIME: 10 MIN   COOK TIME: 30 MIN

WHAT YOU'LL NEED

1 RED BELL PEPPER, SLICED

¾ TSP EXTRA VIRGIN OLIVE OIL

1 (4-OZ) SALMON FILLET

SEA SALT & BLACK PEPPER, TO TASTE

½ CUP SLICED PINEAPPLE

HOW TO MAKE IT

1. Preheat the oven to 400°F and line a baking sheet with parchment paper.
2. In a medium bowl, toss the sliced bell peppers with the olive oil. Transfer to the perimeter of a baking sheet, and add the salmon fillets to the middle.
3. Sprinkle the salmon with salt and pepper, then top with the pineapple slices. Bake for 30 minutes.

MAKES 2 SERVINGS

NUTRITION PER SERVING

263
CALORIES

24g PROTEIN

18g CARBOHYDRATES (4g FIBER)

11g FAT

CHAPTER 6 | The Meal Plan

ONE-PAN LAMB MEATBALLS & VEGGIES

PREP TIME: 10 MIN COOK TIME: 30 MIN

WHAT YOU'LL NEED

12 OZ GROUND LAMB

¾ TSP CHOPPED THYME

1½ MINCED GARLIC CLOVES

⅓ TSP SEA SALT, DIVIDED

2¼ CUPS TRIMMED AND HALVED BRUSSELS SPROUTS

⅓ HEAD CAULIFLOWER, CHOPPED INTO FLORETS

⅓ TSP AVOCADO OIL

HOW TO MAKE IT

1. Heat the oven to 400°F and line a baking sheet with parchment paper.
2. In a medium bowl, combine the lamb, thyme, garlic, and half the sea salt. Mix with your hands until well combined. Roll the mixture into golf ball–size balls and set aside.
3. Add the Brussels sprouts and cauliflower to the pan along with the avocado oil and remaining sea salt. Toss to combine. Place the meatballs on the pan between the veggies. Bake for 30 minutes.

MAKES 2 SERVINGS

NUTRITION PER SERVING

352
CALORIES

22g PROTEIN

10g
CARBOHYDRATES
(4g FIBER)

26g FAT

THE LOSE YOUR GUT GUIDE

ONE-PAN CHICKEN STIR-FRY

PREP TIME: 10 MIN   COOK TIME: 20 MIN

WHAT YOU'LL NEED

2¼ TBSP TAMARI

2¼ TSP APPLE CIDER VINEGAR

2¼ TSP RAW HONEY

2¼ TSP SESAME OIL

1 (15-OZ) CHICKEN BREAST, SLICED INTO CUBES

¾ RED BELL PEPPER, SEEDS REMOVED AND SLICED

¾ YELLOW BELL PEPPER, SEEDS REMOVED AND SLICED

3 CUPS CHOPPED BROCCOLI FLORETS

1½ CUPS SNAP PEAS

½ CUP UNCOOKED QUINOA

1⅛ CUPS WATER

2¼ TSP SESAME SEEDS

HOW TO MAKE IT

1. Preheat the oven to 425°F and line a large baking sheet with parchment paper.

2. In a jar, combine the tamari, apple cider vinegar, honey, and sesame oil. Shake well to combine and set aside.

3. In a large mixing bowl, place the chicken, peppers, broccoli, and snap peas and drizzle with the sauce. Toss to combine, then transfer to the baking sheet. Bake for 25 to 30 minutes, or until chicken is cooked through.

4. Meanwhile, in a saucepan over high heat, cook the quinoa and water. Bring to a boil, then cover with a lid and reduce to a simmer. Let simmer for 12 to 15 minutes, or until all water is absorbed. Remove lid, fluff with a fork, and set aside.

5. Remove chicken and vegetables from the oven and divide into bowls with a side of quinoa. Garnish with sesame seeds. Drizzle with extra tamari or hot sauce if you like.

MAKES 2 SERVINGS

NUTRITION PER SERVING

420

CALORIES

42g PROTEIN

40g CARBOHYDRATES (7g FIBER)

11g FAT

CHAPTER 6 | The Meal Plan

SLOW-COOKER BEEF STEW

PREP TIME: 15 MIN   COOK TIME: 4 HR

WHAT YOU'LL NEED

2 TSP EXTRA VIRGIN OLIVE OIL

10⅔ OZ STEWING BEEF, SLICED INTO BITE-SIZE PIECES

1⅓ TBSP RED WINE VINEGAR

⅔ CUP BABY CARROTS

⅓ SWEET ONION, DICED

¾ CUP MUSHROOMS, SLICED

⅓ CUP BEEF BROTH

⅛ TSP DRIED THYME

⅓ TSP SEA SALT

⅛ TSP BLACK PEPPER

1⅓ TBSP BROWN RICE FLOUR

HOW TO MAKE IT

1. In a slow-cooker, place all ingredients except the brown rice flour and mix well.
2. Cover and cook on low for 4 to 6 hours, or until beef is tender.
3. Remove lid and stir in brown rice flour. Continue to stir until liquid thickens.
4. Ladle into bowls and enjoy!

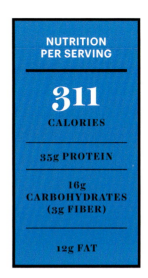

NUTRITION PER SERVING

311 CALORIES

35g PROTEIN

16g CARBOHYDRATES (3g FIBER)

12g FAT

MAKES 2 SERVINGS

THE LOSE YOUR GUT GUIDE

GRILLED SHRIMP SALAD

PREP TIME: 15 MIN   COOK TIME: 10 MIN

NUTRITION PER SERVING

438
CALORIES

48g PROTEIN

15g
CARBOHYDRATES
(7g FIBER)

22g FAT

WHAT YOU'LL NEED

2 TBSP CHOPPED AND PACKED PARSLEY

JUICE OF ¾ LIME

1 TBSP EXTRA VIRGIN OLIVE OIL

⅓ TSP CHILI POWDER

8 OZ RAW, PEELED, AND DEVEINED MEDIUM SHRIMP

1 CUP COLESLAW MIX

¼ CUP HALVED CHERRY TOMATOES

¼ AVOCADO, DICED

SEA SALT & BLACK PEPPER, TO TASTE

HOW TO MAKE IT

1. Make dressing: In a blender or food processor, combine the parsley, lime juice, olive oil, and chili powder. Process until smooth. Set aside.

2. To a resealable food storage bag, add shrimp and half of the dressing. Shake well to coat.

3. Heat a grill or medium skillet. Cook the shrimp for 2 to 3 minutes per side, depending on size of shrimp.

4. Divide coleslaw mix between plates and top with tomatoes, avocado, and grilled shrimp. Season with sea salt and pepper to taste. Drizzle remaining dressing over top.

MAKES 2 SERVINGS

CHAPTER 7 | The Workout

Chapter 7
THE WORKOUT

Remember: The most efficient way to drop pounds (including those around your waist) is with a calculated combo of strength training and cardio. This workout does exactly that. You'll work on building muscle during the first four exercises, then round things out with a couple of heart-pumping, calorie-torching moves. Follow the routine 4 times per week, running for 20 minutes on your rest days, to see results in no time.

Can't perform the routine exactly as shown? Try these tweaks:

- Use a lighter weight.
- Rest a little longer between moves.
- Decrease your reps.

You'll find you get stronger every week, so be sure to adjust your output weekly as well until you are doing the workout as it appears on these pages.

Weekly Workout Schedule

M	T	W	T	F	S	S
WORK	ACTIVE REST WORKOUT	WORK	ACTIVE REST WORKOUT	WORK	ACTIVE REST WORKOUT	WORK

THE LOSE YOUR GUT GUIDE

THE WARMUP

Spiderman Lunge to Thoracic Rotation Start in pushup position, core tight (a), then step your right leg forward, outside your right hand (b). Squeeze your glutes. Lift your right arm and reach toward the ceiling (c); return it to the floor. That's 1 rep; do 2 sets of 10 per side.

THE WORKOUT

Bent-Over Dumbbell Row Stand holding dumbbells at your sides. Push your butt back and hinge forward at the waist until your torso is at a 45-degree angle with the floor. Tighten your core and let the dumbbells hang naturally. This is the start (a). Keeping your core tight, tighten your shoulder blades and row the dumbbells toward your rib cage (b); pause, then lower them. That's 1 rep; do 4 sets of 12 to 15. Rest 90 seconds between sets.

CHAPTER 7 | The Workout

Broomstick Scapular Slide Lie on your stomach, legs straight and arms extended, hands holding a broomstick an inch above the floor. Tighten your shoulder blades and look up slightly (a). Keeping the broomstick off the floor, pull it back to your forehead (b); take 3 seconds to do this. Pause, squeeze your back muscles, then return to the start. That's 1 rep; do 3 sets of 10 to 12. Rest 60 seconds between sets.

FORM TIP
The more you bend at your waist, the easier this gets. Tighten your abs and core so that your torso stays steady throughout each rep.

Eccentric Nordic Curl Kneel on the floor. Brace your feet under a chair or barbell (or have a friend hold your feet), core tight, hands in front. Bend at the waist slightly (a). Tighten your hamstrings and lower your torso to the floor; try to take 5 seconds to do this (b). Place your hands on the floor before your torso hits; press back up. That's 1 rep; do 4 sets of 6.

THE LOSE YOUR GUT GUIDE

Foot-Over Sit on the floor, legs spread apart. Place a dumbbell (or any object) to the left of your right ankle. Sit tall (a). Lift your right leg over the object to the left; gently tap the floor (b), then return to the start. That's 1 rep; do 3 sets of 12 per side.

> **FORM TIP**
> Resist the urge to tip your torso backward. The more upright you sit, the more you'll blast your abs.

Glute Bridge Single-Leg Lower Lie on your back, knees bent, feet flat on the floor and close to your butt. Keeping your core tight, squeeze your glutes, lifting your hips. Straighten your right leg and raise it toward the ceiling. This is the start (a). Slowly lower your right leg, stopping when it is parallel to the floor (b); reverse to the start. That's 1 rep; do 3 sets of 10 per leg.

CHAPTER 7 | The Workout

> **FORM TIP**
>
> *Keep your arms relaxed throughout this drill. You're using the power of your glutes to drive the bell forward.*

THE FINISHER
Dumbbell Swing to Squat Swing

Stand with feet shoulder-width apart, core tight, holding a single dumbbell at your hips with both hands. With your core tight, push your butt back and swing the dumbbell between your legs (a). Stand explosively, squeezing your glutes and driving the dumbbell upward (b). Let its momentum carry it back through your legs (c). This time, propel it upward by sitting back into a squat, keeping your torso upright (d). Alternate reps for 20 seconds, then rest for 10. Do 8 sets.

Chapter 8

THE MIND-SET

Your perspective is probably your most under-utilized weight-loss tool. If you use the tips in chapter 5, you'll keep it focused on the right things from the start. But there is a chance that a bad day or a free plate

CHAPTER 8 | **The Mind-Set**

of frosted donuts might roll around and suddenly the carefully chosen intentions you had a week and a half ago fly right out the window. This doesn't need to be the case. In fact, if you refer to this chapter when those moments appear, you might find that not only are you able to resist the temptation to abandon the plan when things get tough, but that you can do so without breaking a sweat. The more often you employ these tactics, the more it will feel like second nature. So tear these pages out for your fridge or snap a photo to stash on your phone. When you're ready to jump ship, these tips will unfailingly bring you back on course.

5 THINGS TO DO WHEN YOU FEEL LIKE QUITTING

Accept that Your Motivation Isn't High

If you've already been on a weight loss program but you're not as excited about what you're doing as you used to be, the first step to getting your momentum back is actually identifying that your motivation is waning. Sounds obvious, but too many people berate themselves or try to power through this feeling without stopping and noticing that it's happening, and then trying to figure out why it's happening. This doesn't have to be a major investigation. Just ask yourself what's up. What has changed could be something as simple as you don't like going to the grocery store any longer because there's construction on the way and it takes forever to get there. And it can be worked with.

Think Positive

Roll your eyes if you want, but cheesy mantras like "I can do this" really work, research from the UK suggests. In a 2016 study, more than 44,000 participants played an online game using one of three different motivational techniques: reciting a positive mantra, planning out a strategy, and practicing the game in their heads. The roughly 13,000 people who used the mantras—like telling themselves "I can beat my best score"— performed the best in the game, 9 percent better than a control group that didn't use any motivational strategies. That's because the positive pep-talk pumps you up emotionally, says study author Andrew Lane, Ph.D., a

133

THE LOSE YOUR GUT GUIDE

professor of sport psychology at the University of Wolverhampton. Try repeating a mantra in your head, like "I can do this workout" or "I can stick to this meal plan."

Talk It Out

When your mind is saying "screw it," it can be hard to hear any other thoughts in your head. So bring in some outside reinforcements. Text a friend or family member who knows your goals. Let them know you're considering skipping your run or eating that leftover pizza in the fridge. Or join an online community where other people are trying to drop pounds. You'll likely find others in your boat and will be able to learn from their experiences. If you have the money, invest in a nutrition coach. They can help hold you accountable and keep you motivated when you need it most.

Don't forget the power of the perfect playlist. Studies show that music helps boost everything from workout motivation to feelings of confidence.

Check Your Feed (Wisely)

Researchers have found that seeing posts from fitter people led to a more positive outlook. However, not just any social media content will help keep you on track. Checking out gym selfies from your friends might actually demotivate you, according to research. That's because when we compare ourselves to people we can closely identify with, we often find ways in which we're lacking. So, if you need some motivation to tackle your workout, scroll through posts from fit people who inspire you but maybe aren't contacts in your phone.

Break Your Goal Into Smaller Pieces

When you're staring down the vending machine at 3 p.m., your main goal of losing weight can seem pretty distant. You might think one bag of chips doesn't have much impact on what you're ultimately trying to achieve. But adjusting your mindset to view your big goal as a series of smaller goals can help you see the importance of smaller decisions. Your big goal might be losing weight, but the smaller goals that will make it happen include avoiding empty calories and making an effort to move more.

ABOUT THE AUTHOR

Dezi Abeyta, RDN, is a proud husband, father, and a Latino dietitian entrepreneur for his online nutrition business Foodtalk Nutrition. Dezi has creatively branded himself as the go-to nutrition coach for dads and families. Follow him on Instagram @fitdadscoach. His mission is to empower his fellow "Man of Purpose" to become better health role models for themselves, first, and then for their families. Dezi has also been a consulting dietitian for Major League Baseball (MLB) and enjoys the positive impact that he has had not only in the male community but also as a TEDx speaker. You can find his talk, "Food Fights Can Save Your Life," on YouTube, where he discusses the parallels between the development of healthy relationships with food and how to feed your children. The best way to connect with him is to join his free and private O.P.N. Facebook Community for Parents!

THANK YOU

FOR PURCHASING THE LOSE YOUR GUT GUIDE

Boost your health and fitness with more from *Men's Health*!
Visit our online store and **save 20% off your first purchase.**

 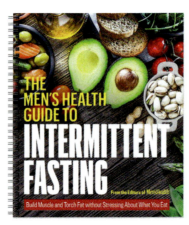 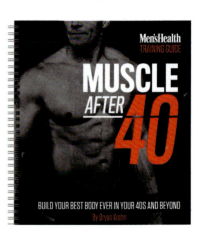

PLEASE ENJOY 20% OFF AT OUR STORE!

20% OFF

USE COUPON CODE THANKYOU20

Shop.MensHealth.com

Offer only applies to books, guides, DVDs, and new magazine subscription purchases and is not eligible on Airbnb and Pioneer Woman Magazine. Additional restrictions may apply.